Four (and a half) Dialogues on Homosexuality and the Bible

Four (and a half) Dialogues on Homosexuality and the Bible

BY

Donald J. Zeyl

FOREWORD BY *Nicholas P. Wolterstorff*

CASCADE *Books* · Eugene, Oregon

Cascade Books
An Imprint of Wipf and Stock Publishers
199 W. 8th Ave., Suite 3
Eugene, OR 97401

www.wipfandstock.com

PAPERBACK ISBN: 978-1-6667-1502-6
HARDCOVER ISBN: 978-1-6667-1503-3
EBOOK ISBN: 978-1-6667-1504-0

Cataloguing-in-Publication data:

Names: Zeyl, Donald J.
Title: Four (and a half) dialogues on homosexuality and the Bible / Donald J. Zeyl.
Description: Eugene, OR: Cascade Books, 2022 | Includes bibliographical references.
Identifiers: ISBN 978-1-6667-1502-6 (paperback) | ISBN 978-1-6667-1503-3 (hardcover) | ISBN 978-1-6667-1504-0 (ebook)
Subjects: LCSH: Homosexuality—Biblical teaching. | Bible and homosexuality. | Homosexuality—Religious aspects—Christianity—United States.
Classification: BS680.H67 Z49 2022 (print) | BS680.H67 (ebook)

To the Memory of

Remkes Kooistra

and

Lewis B. Smedes

"Get Used to Different."

—JESUS, character in *THE CHOSEN*,
Season One, Episode 7

Contents

Foreword

DISAGREEMENTS ABOUT WHAT THE Bible teaches concerning the morality of same-sex marriage have been roiling in the Christian community for decades: families have been torn apart, denominations split, scheduled speakers disinvited, books pulled off shelves, financial support for organizations withdrawn, persons removed from boards, irate charges exchanged.

Into this maelstrom comes Donald Zeyl's *Four (and a half) Dialogues on Homosexuality and the Bible* as a healing balm. Rather than adding one more voice to the cacophony, it presents four Christian college students: close friends, two women, two men, of different sexual orientations and with differing interpretations of Scripture, listening empathetically to each other's life-stories and attending to each other's biblical interpretations, carefully explaining where and why they disagree, when they do, never dismissing a friend's interpretation as simply wrong-headed. Their dialogue is a compelling model for how to discuss this volatile issue openly, honestly, and lovingly.

The participants speak frankly about their sexual orientation: two are gay, two are straight. Those who are gay narrate vividly the turmoil they experienced in realizing that they were gay, and the hurt they experienced in "coming out" to family, friends, and church. They describe how they are now living out their same-sex orientation, one as committed to lifelong celibacy, the other as planning to get married.

None of the participants is reduced to just a sexual being, however. We come to know them as persons—Amanda as straightforward, to the point sometimes of being blunt, Philip as a bit breezy, David as philosophical, befitting a philosophy major, and Stephanie as organized and organizer. These are not puppets mouthing intellectual positions, as is the case for some of Plato's dialogues. These are individuals of distinct personalities with different sexual orientations exchanging views concerning what they understand the Bible to be teaching concerning the morality of same-sex marriage.

They are genuinely conversing, not simply delivering set speeches. *Four (and a half) Dialogues* is a literary achievement.

Their conversation is not a dispassionate scholarly discussion concerning matters of biblical interpretation. What the Bible teaches on the topic under discussion is, for them, of existential importance. For them, Scripture is authoritative. What they understand Scripture to be teaching shapes their lives—not always easily—and shapes the advice they give their friends.

Amanda and David are led by their interpretation of Scripture to a "non-affirming" position on the morality of same-sex marriage; Philip and Stephanie, to an "affirming" position. Within each pair, however, the positions held are supported by quite different biblical interpretations. Thus: four distinctly different positions on what Scripture teaches concerning the morality of same-sex marriage.

The positions held by Amanda, David, and Philip can all be found, in their general outlines, in the now-voluminous literature on the issue of Scripture and same-sex marriage. Each of them gives their own particular "twist" to the general position, however. They present their position compellingly, and support it with insightful, sometimes novel, biblical interpretations. Philip's interpretation of what Paul was saying in the first chapter of *Romans* is remarkably perceptive. In the case of Stephanie, hers is a neo-progressive view that I have not previously encountered, and that I find compelling.

The discussion among the participants proves to be, thus, an extended lesson in how to interpret and apply Scripture. Familiar passages are given fresh interpretations, and passages that have seldom, if ever, been brought into the discussion are shown to be surprisingly relevant. The author is a professional philosopher whose specialty is ancient philosophy. His linguistic and hermeneutical skills are here put to admirable use, as is his broad knowledge of Scripture and of the extensive literature on the topic.

Four (and a half) Dialogues is a model for how to discuss this contentious issue openly, honestly, and lovingly. It's a lesson in how to interpret Scripture and how to embody Scripture in one's life. And its biblical interpretations represent a significant advance in discussion of the issues. May its readers be many!

Nicholas P. Wolterstorff
Noah Porter Professor Emeritus of Philosophical Theology, Yale University
Senior Research Fellow, Institute for Advanced Studies in Culture,
   University of Virginia

Acknowledgments

THIS BOOK IS THE product of several years of prayerful reading, discussion, and reflection on the issue debated in this book. Among those who interacted with me I want to thank in particular my friend Nathan Albert, who served as youth pastor in my local church at the time my basic perspective was coming together. Nathan partnered with me during a difficult time in our respective church leadership roles, and our periodic lunches together were mutually encouraging.

I am grateful to many who have read the manuscript in its various stages of development, in whole or in part, and offered helpful feedback, both critical and constructive, as well as encouragement. These include Roger Dewey, Karen Keene, William Loader, my nephew Derek Zeyl, and my brother Thomas Zeyl. In particular I want to thank my pastor Vann Trapp, whose critique at several points forced me to clarify and express my ideas with greater nuance. I'm very grateful to my friend and former student Gregory Ganssle for pointing out that turtles are not amphibians and suggesting salamanders instead; and for a number of other astute observations, critiques and suggestions. Thanks to my friend Jennifer Morison Hendrix for her amazing editorial skills, her perceptive engagement with the text, and follow-up video discussions. Finally, my thanks to David Gushee for supporting the project and helping to connect me with the publisher, and to Nicholas Wolterstorff for providing such a perceptive, eloquent, and generous foreword.

This book is dedicated to the memory of two pastor-teachers who awakened my thinking about the issue of same-sex relationships. Remkes Kooistra (1917–2005) was my pastor at First Toronto CRC during my undergraduate years at the University of Toronto in the mid-nineteen sixties. He was the first to raise my awareness of the issue when he wrote, "God allows homosexuals to be sexually active within the same bonds of morality that limit heterosexual activity. It's my honest opinion. I believe there should be some room for discussion on these theological issues."[1] I hope that this book goes some way to respond to his proposal. Lewis B. Smedes (1921–2002), the better-known author of *Sex for Christians: The Limits and Liberties of Sexual Living* (revised edition, 1994), offered a concise, eloquent, and compassionate defense of same-sex relationships that I found and still find compelling (pp. 238–44).

---

1. Published in *Christian Courier*, date unknown, and cited in the on-line newsletter of *Evangelicals Concerned, Inc.*, Spring 1997. http://ecinc.org/record-newsletter/spring-1997-2/.

Introduction

March 24, 2014: World Vision, one of America's largest Christian charities, announces a policy change that will permit gay Christians in legal same-sex marriages to be employed in its organization. **March 26, 2014:** World Vision reverses its decision to hire Christians in same-sex marriages.

What happened?

July 12, 2017: Eugene Peterson, a prominent and much loved pastor-teacher, prolific and influential author, hesitantly tells an interviewer that if asked, he would agree to officiate at a same-sex wedding. **July 13, 2017:** Eugene Peterson retracts his answer to the interviewer's question.

What happened?

Evangelical outrage is what happened. *Christianity Today* described it as "heavy backlash from the evangelical community."[1] A chorus of prominent evangelical leaders denounced World Vision's policy change. Some denominational leaders called on their members to cancel their World Vision sponsorships of children in the developing world, seemingly indifferent to the jeopardy they would thereby bring upon these already vulnerable children. And Lifeway Christian Stores, America's largest Christian retail chain, was poised to pull from its shelves all titles authored by Eugene Peterson, including his highly popular *The Message*. A *CT* commentator diagnosed Peterson's state of mind as "theological indifference" which, he

---

1. "World Vision Reverses Decision To Hire Christians in Same-Sex Marriages." March 26, 2014. https://www.christianitytoday.com/ct/2014/march-web-only/world-vision-reverses-decision-gay-same-sex-marriage.html.

opined, is "worse than progressivism."[2] On both occasions, an earthquake rocked the evangelical world—outrage from a disapproving majority and consternation from a sympathetic minority.

These two events, one prior and the other subsequent to the federal legalization of same-sex marriage in the United States, attest to the fact that opposition to same-sex marriage remains a defining mark of evangelical identity. Several denominations with an evangelical heritage and witness experience strain and disquiet within their ranks. LGBTQ+ lobby groups such as "All One Body" in my denomination of origin, the Christian Reformed Church, and "Mission Friends 4 Inclusion" in my current denomination, the Evangelical Covenant Church, have organized as voices of protest and lament against policies that they perceive to be exclusionary. The leaders of these denominations in their turn wrestle with their own consciences and understandings of Scripture, and agonize over the threat of factionalism and secession by member congregations, and so for the most part continue to resist the pull that these lobby groups exert. Their highest deliberative assemblies are obliged to cast votes that some participants applaud and others lament.

At issue is the question of whether the Bible permits same-sex marriage and thus whether same-sex monogamous relationships may be viewed as blessed by God and therefore to be affirmed by the church. The contrary answers given to this question line up individuals, congregations and denominations into opposing camps: "conservatives" or "traditionalists" against "progressives" or "liberals." Tensions rise, votes are taken, and, sadly, organizational splits occur, often with attendant disputes over name and property rights. Each side tends to oversimplify, even caricature, the position of the other. Progressives accuse traditionalists of valuing law above love, theological abstraction above the lives of real people, and traditionalists accuse progressives of forsaking the Bible and capitulating to a secular agenda. Eventually dialogue comes to a halt, and each side ends up listening only to its own voice.

Evangelical cancel culture is alive and well. Authors and speakers who change their minds from a non-affirming to an affirming stance are censured and their voices silenced. They are disinvited from speaking engagements at evangelical venues, their names disappear from the mastheads of evangelical organizations, and their books are pulled from the shelves of

---

2. "Eugene Peterson Shrugs." July 13, 2017. https://www.christianitytoday.com/ct/2017/july-web-only/eugene-peterson-shrugs.html.

evangelical bookstores. A difference in viewpoint on what might reasonably be regarded as one of a number of "non-essential" doctrinal issues over which evangelical Christians of different persuasions have historically disagreed (as they have about baptism, charismatic gifts, eschatology, the role of women in church and marriage, and, more recently, creation and evolution) is not to be tolerated on this issue. Liberty of conscience, once a fundamental principle of the Protestant reformation, is not permitted here. To affirm same-sex marriage is to embrace heresy, to place oneself beyond the pale of evangelical orthodoxy.

It is in this context of tension and unrest that I offer these dialogues as a platform for learning and discussion. The issue of LGBTQ+ inclusion in the body of Christ is a defining issue for our time and if it is not addressed and resolved well, it will continue to undermine evangelical life and witness for generations to come. I wrote these dialogues as an exercise in imagining what an extended conversation among Christian friends might look like—friends who differ in sexual orientation and theological perspectives relating to the issues of homosexuality and same-sex marriage—and how they might handle their differences. My inspiration has been the hope that these dialogues might nurture a better conversation among people of evangelical conviction. Additionally, I hope that they will promote a deeper engagement with the (relatively few) biblical texts that speak to this issue. I have been dissatisfied with the lack of depth and focus in biblical interpretation on both sides, especially in the interpretation of Romans 1:18–27. Too many pertinent questions about this passage remain unasked, let alone unanswered.

The dialogue form is the oldest literary form for engaging philosophical and theological topics in Western thought, beginning with Plato in the fourth century BCE. Rather than advocating some definite point of view, this form facilitates the exploration of multiple perspectives on some issue of interest and does not attempt to coerce readers into taking any particular side. It draws readers into the conversation and invites them to evaluate for themselves the strength of the various arguments presented, so as to come to their own conclusions. Great thinkers from Plato to Cicero, Augustine, and Hume have employed this literary form to excellent effect. Of course these authors are not neutral on the topics they discuss, and I do not pretend to be neutral on the issue debated in this book. The best I can hope for is that I have been fair, objective, and sympathetic to all viewpoints, including those with which I disagree. I hope that my readers will share a similar posture.

The dialogues are designed for group study and discussion, but will also be of benefit to individuals who prefer to reflect on the subject matter on their own. I have tried to provide balance to these conversations. Two of the four characters are male and two are female. Two are straight and two are gay. Two defend an "affirming" answer to the question of same-sex marriage and two defend a "non-affirming" answer. It should be noted that the two affirming perspectives are distinct from each other in important ways, as are the two non-affirming ones. So four distinct points of view are examined. For those who like labels (which I have avoided in composing these conversations), they could be described—in the order in which they are taken up—as "conservative" (Amanda, first dialogue), "progressive" (Philip, second dialogue), "neo-conservative" (David, third dialogue) and "neo-progressive" (Stephanie, fourth dialogue).

The conversations include not just the back and forth of theological and biblical arguments but also the characters' stories of their experiences with their sexuality. Like the characters themselves, these stories are fictional, though they incorporate real life elements. The stories serve to remind us that homosexuality is not just an abstract theological "issue" on which we are urged to take a "position" but a deeply personal experience for countless individuals who seek to follow Christ and honor him in their lives.

The first dialogue sets the table for the conversations to follow. It is probably the position that is most familiar to readers of this book, since it represents the way the Bible has historically been read and applied by the church. In recent times this position has been articulated succinctly by the "Nashville Statement." That statement has been criticized (rightly, in my view) for its strident, combative tone. Tone aside, the Nashville Statement aptly summarizes the traditional conservative position on the issue.

The other dialogues are in their various ways responses to this position. The second dialogue presents a perspective that is at furthest remove from it. This perspective, which I've called "progressive," charges the conservative position with either misreading or misapplying the biblical texts upon which it is based. It offers alternative readings of those texts to support a conclusion that the Bible neither condemns nor disallows same-sex relationships or marriage—in fact, the Bible implicitly supports it and therefore, its proponents argue, this position should be embraced by the church.

The neo-conservative position rejects the defense of same-sex relationships and marriage proposed in the second dialogue, yet is more open than the traditional conservative position to the accounts of homosexuality as a psychological and even biological phenomenon developed in recent decades through scientific research. It concludes that while the Bible clearly condemns as sinful all same-sex behavior (and so by implication all relationships that include such behavior), it does not condemn same-sex attraction as such, which is an unchosen condition of many individuals, hardwired into their psychophysical make-up. And while the traditional conservative position tends to reject the use of labels such as "gay" or "lesbian" to describe Christian same-sex attracted individuals, those holding the neo-conservative point of view for the most part endorse the use of such labels.

Finally, what I've called the "neo-progressive" position, introduced in the fourth dialogue, has to the best of my knowledge not previously been represented in the literature. This position agrees with the two conservative positions that the Bible's account of God's design for gender, sexuality, and marriage is heteronormative. On the other hand, it also argues that God sometimes creates individuals in ways that do not align with that design. This raises the question of whether God's will for human sexual relationships always and invariably follows God's design or whether God's requirements for such relationships may be "accommodated" to the way God actually creates people. This position, then, combines the affirmation of traditional biblical norms for gender, sexuality, and marriage in general with openness to the permissibility of same-sex relationships and marriage for those whom God has created in a way that is not in alignment with those norms. I believe that this hybrid position, more than any of the others, promises a way forward out of the current impasse. It is consistent with contemporary evangelical approaches to biblical interpretation as well as expressive of the empathy, generosity, and hospitality that Christians are called to exercise toward one another and indeed to all people, especially to those who are marginalized by society and even by the church. Whether the claims and arguments made on behalf of this position are plausible I leave to my readers to decide.

These four positions, then, are held in tension with each other as the conversations move forward. That tension is not resolved nor is it the intent of the dialogues to resolve it. There is, I am convinced, room for disagreement. My main purpose in writing the dialogues is to foster what has been called "generous spaciousness"[3] on this issue. The concluding dialogue (the "half dialogue") wrestles with the question of how that spaciousness might be worked out in a way that "preserves the unity of the Spirit in the bond of peace" (Ephesians 4:3) within the context of Christian communities.

The conversations range over questions such as these:

- What is homosexuality? How do we understand it biologically? How do we understand it theologically—i.e., how does it relate to God's "creation order"? How does it relate to "the fall"?

- Do the biblical texts that prohibit homosexual activity reflect cultural situations or do they reflect a universal divine design?

- How, in particular, should we understand the condemnation of homosexuality in Romans 1? What are the theological, rhetorical and historical contexts of that condemnation? Why should an awareness of those contexts matter?

- What exactly is meant by the characterizations of homosexuality in that chapter as (i) involving an "exchange" and (ii) being "contrary to nature"?

- Does an accurate reading of Romans 1 accommodate a distinction between (supposedly non-culpable) same-sex attraction and (culpable) same-sex lusts and passions, as is sometimes claimed?

- Our current knowledge of homosexuality is different from that of the biblical authors and their contemporaries. Should that make a difference in our theological and ethical appraisal of same-sex relationships and marriage?

- Is there good reason, biblical or theological, to believe that God creates some people gay?

- Is same-sex "marriage" really *marriage*?

These are for the most part open-ended questions about which well intentioned Christians who agree in accepting the Bible's authority might well find themselves in disagreement with one another. Our opinions are

3. See Wendy Vanderwal–Gritter, *Generous Spaciousness: Responding to Gay Christians in the Church.* Grand Rapid: Brazos, 2014.

often colored by our own experiences and backgrounds, and all of us are to some degree resistant to ideas that take us out of our comfort zones. Honest conversations around this topic are hard—and risky! They can be undertaken only in a spirit of prayer and in humble dependence on the Holy Spirit. I am convinced that such conversations can succeed and bear fruit for the church if only we will open both our minds and our hearts to one another's stories and ways of engaging Scripture.

May God bless and honor our attempts to wrestle with his Word and discern his will for us as a diverse community of believers on this very sensitive but hugely significant subject.

Don Zeyl
June 2021

Prologue

STEPHANIE: Hi there. My name is Stephanie and I'm a senior, majoring in Classics at a well-known liberal arts college in the mid-western United States. I'm a Christian, and am part of the Campus Christian Fellowship at my college. It is there that I met David, Amanda, and Philip. Besides attending the weekly Large Group meeting of the Fellowship, we are also in the same Bible study together. Over the course of the last several years we've become really good friends.

It so happens that two of us are straight and two are gay. The subject of homosexuality has occasionally come up in our conversations, both within and outside of our Bible study meetings. It has become apparent that we differ in our views on this subject, especially as to how it relates to the Bible. All four of us are committed to the Bible's authority and to living our lives under its authority, yet we understand the Bible's message differently and are in different places on the issue. Our shared desire to understand each other better led to a decision that we should make time to discuss our respective views at length, defending them biblically and allowing the others to question them. So, last fall we met on four consecutive Friday nights. In each of these sessions one of us would begin by telling the others his or her story of how their life was impacted by homosexuality, and go on to present a "case" for their view. The others would be free to ask questions or interject comments. Our aim was not so much to achieve consensus on this issue—though if that were to happen, it would certainly be a bonus—but to hear one another clearly, to remove any misconceptions we might have about our various positions, and to discover for ourselves whether this is a subject we can talk about honestly and respectfully, without pronouncing judgment on one another's views.

After we had concluded our series of conversations it occurred to us that others might benefit from listening in, so we came together several times during the following months to create a transcript of our conversations. We pooled our recollections, refined our thoughts and occasionally reshaped the drift of our conversations. We settled on a draft that satisfied each one of us and found a publisher who accepted our manuscript for publication. We're pleased to offer the final product to you. We chose the English Standard Version (ESV) translation of the Bible because it professes to be an "essentially literal" translation and because it is widely accepted as reliable in the Christian communities we represent.

Our hope and prayer for you, as you read and reflect on these conversations, is that you will participate. Our aim in sharing them with you is not so much to persuade you to adopt any particular point of view as to hold up a mirror to you. Pay close attention to any thoughts or feelings that arise in you as you process the ideas we present. Ask yourself why you are thinking or feeling as you do about some idea or suggestion one of us makes. How would *you* respond to that suggestion and why would you respond that way? What are your fears or dreams as you think about the subject of homosexuality, especially in the context of Christian community? Are you really open to reconsidering your own beliefs and being more hospitable to the beliefs of others? Pray for the Holy Spirit to guide you as you listen to your heart.

Our prayer is that God will use these conversations to help heal the deep divisions that now characterize the wider conservative Christian community. That community is not at peace, and conflicts over the subject of homosexuality and the Bible have been erupting in many places for many decades. These conflicts seem to be intensifying in our day. If you are part of a church or other Christian community that finds it hard to talk about this issue, you might want to consider recommending this book to launch a conversation.

Jesus calls his church not to conflict but to peace (Mark 9:50). Amanda, David, Philip, and I ask you to join us in seeking the mind of Christ and his will for his church.

Oh, one more thing. You'll notice that there are many times when one of us puts an idea on the table that gets an initial response from one or two of the others, but the idea isn't developed and thoroughly discussed until much later. That's because the idea isn't quite ripe for full discussion until other related ideas have been examined. So please don't assume that we are done with a particular idea until the end of our last conversation.

Finally, we follow tradition in referring to God by using masculine pronouns. We acknowledge that God is without or perhaps beyond gender, but the avoidance of pronouns in referring to God is stylistically cumbersome and worse, distracting. We apologize in advance.

Nice to meet you! Please join us in our cycle of conversations.

Dialogue 1

It is a quiet October Friday night on campus. After dinner together in one of the college's dining halls, Amanda, David, Philip, and Stephanie make their way to one of the adjoining common rooms for coffee and conversation. Tonight's conversation will be the first of a series that the participants planned several weeks before, not long after they reunited with one another at the school year's kick-off meeting of the Campus Christian Fellowship.

STEPHANIE: Hey guys, I'm glad we could all make it tonight. I've looked forward to these conversations ever since we agreed to have them. We all have different views on the subject of homosexuality and the Bible, but I'm glad that we're friends despite these differences. I really hope we'll remain so, whether we come to points of agreement or not. After all, our common connection as Christians, committed followers of Jesus Christ, and our shared desire to live God-pleasing lives, far exceed any theological differences we may have. I'm glad we also all believe that it is far better to try to talk through our differences than build up silos around our individual points of view. We may or may not find common ground. But even if we don't, it is far better to have heard each other out. I am sure that we'll all learn *something* from our discussion, whether or not we succeed in changing anyone else's mind.

PHILIP: Thanks, Stephanie, for organizing this series. I am so tired of the boxes we Christians put each other into. My hope is that as we discuss and debate, we can all be totally honest and open with one another, and enter into a spirit of truly listening and learning, rather than passing judgment. This has to do not only with learning how to understand and apply the Bible correctly—and I totally agree that that's a non-negotiable priority—but also with being able to enter into one another's lives, seeing life through the eyes of people who are different from ourselves.

Stephanie: Great point, Phil. We've agreed that we should proceed by each of us first telling our story on the subject—how we came to discover that we are gay or straight, what difficulties, if any, this presented for us, how our faith in Christ was impacted, and how we are doing today with our sexuality as we currently experience it—and second, explaining how each of us sees the Bible speaking to issues of sexuality and marriage, including same-sex marriage. We'll give each other the freedom to ask questions or make comments as our presentations move along. Are we all good with this?

David: I'm fine with this, but I think we need to start with prayer. We can't expect to discuss this topic in our own wisdom and strength. We need the Holy Spirit to guide us. Is it okay if I pray? *All murmur agreement. David continues.*

> *Holy Spirit, we humbly acknowledge that we need you. You are the Spirit of Truth who, Jesus promised, would guide us into all Truth. We pray that you would open the eyes of our understanding and, as we listen to each other's stories and examine how each of us hears your Word, that we would not be motivated by the desire to prove ourselves right, but to learn from one another's insights and experiences. In particular, we pray for those of us and any of our friends who experience same-sex attractions—especially our brothers and sisters in Christ—that you would relieve them of any burdens they may be carrying, and that whatever the outcome of our conversations, they will feel loved by you and your people. In Jesus's precious name, Amen.*

Stephanie: Okay, as we've agreed, Amanda will start us off tonight, followed next week by Philip. Then, the following week, David and finally, three weeks from tonight, myself. This will be the most natural progression. Are you ready to begin, Amanda?

Amanda: I am. So here's my story. As all of you know, I am a same-sex attracted female. I won't call myself "gay," or "lesbian," but I certainly understand why folks who know of my attraction will put those labels on me. The reason I reject the labels is that I don't believe that I have a gay or lesbian *identity*, which is what is suggested by the use of these labels. My identity is that I am a child of God, born to new life in Jesus Christ. I did not always have that identity. I grew up in what I would call a secular progressive home. My parents are atheists. They had no interest in taking me to any church. Their view was that churches, particularly those they called "fundamentalist," were a bigoted and regressive force in our society, to be tolerated, perhaps, but best to be avoided. So when as a kid I discovered my sexual attraction to other girls and the absence of any attraction to boys, my parents were totally fine with it! They even hosted a "coming out" party for me to which they invited all their progressively minded friends, who effusively affirmed and congratulated me.

DAVID: Amanda, I'm struck by your not wanting to identify yourself as gay or lesbian. I totally agree that your new life in Christ is your basic, your ultimate identity, but that doesn't seem to me to rule out that at a very deep, if not ultimate, level you are a gay person. After all, your being same-sex attracted isn't just an incidental fact about you, like your preference for tea over coffee, but a deep aspect of who you really are, of what makes you *you*. It seems to me that you are resisting, refusing to accept, a really basic fact about yourself. I don't want to debate this now, but I do think that this is an issue we should take up later.

PHILIP: I'm glad you picked up on that, Dave. This is important to me, too.

AMANDA: If I were to *identify* myself as gay, I would be accepting as normal and essential to who I am something about me that is deeply broken. 2 Corinthians 5:17 declares that I am a "new creation" in Christ. My new identity in Christ assures me that God sees me as a completely new and whole person, not as a broken sinner.

DAVID: I understand that and don't disagree. But I believe that there's more to be said about this complex issue of one's sexual identity. I'll wait until it's my turn to elaborate on that. Please go on with your story, Amanda.

AMANDA: Okay. So, when I entered high school, I discovered to my great delight that there were other girls at school who also were attracted to girls, and it didn't take long before we found each other and were hooking up together. I'm ashamed to think of it now, but at the time I hadn't the vaguest idea that that was wrong. Why should it be? It felt good and we weren't hurting anybody. This went on for a couple of years, but then in my junior year I fell head over heels in love with a young woman. Her name was Sarah, and she reciprocated my love for her. Sarah took my breath away. She was beautiful, smart, and kind. I longed for a life of love with her. We established a relationship that went far beyond any hookups. The Supreme Court hadn't yet legalized same-sex marriage at that time, and it wasn't yet legal in our state, but Sarah and I were sure we wanted to get married once it became legal.

Then something happened near the end of my senior year. Even though I had a thoroughly secular upbringing, I had begun to wonder about God, death, and eternity. What if my well-educated parents, liberal to the point of condescension, were wrong about religion? What if there really is a God? What if there really is an eternal afterlife? Much as I tried, I could not stifle these questions. One of my friends at school was a boy who had shared his faith in Christ with me on several occasions. At first I found this funny and humored him, but since I liked him as a friend, I didn't shut him down. Maybe my questions grew out of conversations with him; I don't remember. At any rate, he invited me to go on a weekend retreat with the youth group from his church. I laughed it off at first, but the idea kept growing on me, and eventually I accepted. I told my parents some lie or other and boarded the bus to the retreat site.

One of the speakers at this retreat raised the question, "What are you living for?" He proclaimed with great conviction that yes, there is a God, and yes, God had created me, and again yes, the fulfillment of my life could only come about when I surrendered my will to God's and lived out God's purpose for my life. But for this to be possible I had to be reconciled to God, and this could only happen if I accepted Jesus's sacrifice on the cross for my sins. He explained what I needed to do to accept Jesus, and as he finished his talk, he invited all those who had accepted Jesus just then to come forward and be prayed over. With fear and trembling I went forward. I still didn't understand clearly, but I was overwhelmed by the realization that this was a unique moment, and if I walked away, I might not have this opportunity again. Along with several others I prayed a prayer that acknowledged that I was a sinner, that Jesus had died for my sins, and that I would turn my life over to him. I had made a "decision for Christ," as many folks describe it. I found an immediate peace coming over me that confirmed I had done the right thing. So now all of my sins were forgiven, and I had a completely new life—a new identity.

My parents were very upset with my conversion. They felt that I had gone over to the dark side, allying myself with the culturally narrow-minded and bigoted. They warned me that "homophobia" was rampant in "those kinds of churches," and told me that they were confident it wouldn't take me long to get over my delusion.

Shortly afterward Pastor Kevin, the youth pastor at my friend's church, asked to meet with me. He had learned that I had accepted Christ, and he also knew that I was in an active same-sex relationship. With great kindness and patience he began a conversation with me about my sexuality. He asked me if I was open to finding out what the Bible has to say about homosexuality. Hesitant, I said yes. So he opened up his Bible and pointed out that in the beginning God created humans as male and female as an expression of his image, and designed sex between them not only as a means of procreation, but also as an expression of intimate love between them. He pointed out as gently as he could that sex between two women or two men is contrary to God's design, a violation of God's creation order, and therefore sinful. He read aloud several passages in the Bible that condemned homosexual behavior as sinful, abominable to God, and the consequence of human rebellion against God. Those who engage in same-sex behavior are excluded from the kingdom of God. He gently but urgently pointed out that I had a choice to make. It came down to this: if I was serious about following Christ, I needed to break off my relationship with Sarah.

PHILIP: It sounds like Pastor Kevin might not have been aware that his theology is controversial. Did he give any indication that he was basing his counsel to you on a particular *interpretation* of the Bible—one that has held long sway in the history of the church—or did he simply tell you that this is what the Bible says?

AMANDA: No, he gave no hint that the Bible passages he cited were open to interpretation, let alone to any interpretation that might have allowed for other choices I could make.

STEPHANIE: Well, that's why we're here, to try to sort this out for ourselves. Anyhow, Amanda, please go on with your story.

AMANDA: I don't remember exactly what I said to Pastor Kevin when I heard that, but I left that meeting in a flood of tears. I was devastated. I could not see how I could possibly give up my relationship with Sarah. Our love was too strong. I cried all that first night. Was God really asking me to give up something that was so precious to me? Was what Pastor Kevin had said about God's design and same-sex relationships being contrary to that design and therefore sinful really in the Bible? And was it really true? I had to know.

Through my tears, I also prayed. "God," I cried out, "What are you asking me to do? I cannot do this! Yet you want to be first in my life. You have the right to be first in my life. I get that, and very deep down that's what I want too! I cannot do this on my own, and the thought just kills me. Please help me!"

Almost immediately God answered my prayer very clearly and very powerfully. I will never forget it. I could hear deep within me the voice of God audibly speaking to me, telling me that not only was my history of sexual behavior sinful in his holy sight, but also that my same-sex attractions were contrary to how he had created me. God called me to repentance and assured me of his unconditional, overwhelming love for me, and his total forgiveness of all my sin. I clearly heard him call me to end my relationship with Sarah and break once and for all with my same-sex past.

DAVID: I hesitate to bring up this point, Amanda, because I don't want to disrespect your account of how you experienced God's answer to your prayer. You clearly are convinced that it was God who spoke to you, and I don't have a right to undermine that conviction. Yet I have to tell you that I'm skeptical. There have been many times throughout church history when individuals claimed to be certain they heard a message from God that turned out to be false and ended up misleading many people. I'm not saying that God can't or doesn't communicate that way—clearly he did in biblical times. Nor am I saying that on this occasion God didn't speak to you. How could I know that? All I'm saying is that your certainty about your experience doesn't transfer to me.

STEPHANIE: Subjective experiences of God speaking to a particular person need to be measured against an objective, authoritative standard. For Christians the Bible is that standard. But what the Bible teaches about homosexuality is open to debate, as Phil pointed out just now. Your experience of hearing God speaking to you comes in the wake of your hearing Pastor Kevin's account of a handful of biblical passages—passages that we ourselves will be examining closely over the course of the next several weeks.

PHILIP: I'm more than skeptical about your experience, Amanda. To be totally frank, I seriously doubt that you heard from God at all. As I'll be sharing later, the experiences I've had with God leading my life in the area of my sexuality take me in a very different direction. I'll be sharing those experiences when my turn comes up. But I will admit in advance that the caveat Dave and Steph applied to you will have to apply to me as well. Please go on, Amanda.

AMANDA: I respect your point of view, guys, but it doesn't diminish my conviction that God really did speak to me. So, convinced of that as I was, I did what God called me to do. The actual break-up with Sarah was incredibly painful. Both of us were in tears. "How can you do this to us!" I tried to explain to her that my life and priorities were under new management now that I had become a Christian. She did not understand. I said goodbye and broke off all contact with Sarah. Eventually Sarah accepted our break up, and we've both moved on. I learned recently that she is in a new relationship with another woman now. But I have to admit that it took a long time for my heart to heal.

Neither my prayer for God's help, nor God's answer to my prayer, nor the break-up with Sarah ended my feelings of attraction to other women, however. This troubled me greatly, so I asked for another meeting with Pastor Kevin. I shared with him my break-up with Sarah, and my decision to never again involve myself in sex with other women. I told him I had expected God to honor that decision by taking away my attraction to women and, maybe, hopefully, giving me an attraction to men. This did not happen!

Pastor Kevin listened sympathetically. After a while, he said, "It's very rare that same-sex attractions disappear immediately upon conversion, though that does sometimes happen. Did you know that there is help for you? There are organizations, many of them Christian, that have been formed to help same-sex attracted individuals to overcome their attractions. These organizations have developed what is called 'reparative therapy' or 'conversion therapy.' From what I hear, they are quite successful in helping gay and lesbian people abandon a gay life style, and many who have gone through their programs are now happily married with kids. If you are interested, I can help connect you with some of them that have an office here locally."

PHILIP: Did you go?

AMANDA: Yes, I did. There was an organization with an international reach that was right in my hometown. I signed up and went through their program. My parents went ballistic when they found out. They denounced it with language like "fake science," "brainwashing," and so on. "You're fine the way you are!" For a while they refused to speak to me.

PHILIP: How did the program work out for you?

AMANDA: I wish I could tell you that my same-sex attractions eventually vanished. That's what I kept hoping and praying for. I was crushed when this did not happen. What is wrong with me? My desires for sexual intimacy with women are as alive in me now as ever before. The program was somewhat helpful in reinforcing my decision to leave a life of same-sex involvement, but it definitely did not reduce my same-sex desires.

PHILIP: I'm not surprised, Amanda. Your experience is by far more the rule than the exception. Your parents are better informed about so called "reparative therapy" than Christians like Pastor Kevin. So how are you dealing with your same-sex desires?

AMANDA: I can't control them, but I don't have to own them. Whenever I experience a moment of sexual attraction to another woman, I have learned to nip it in the bud. I'm not saying this nipping is easy and that this isn't a daily struggle for me. These moments are part of my "old self," my "flesh," that I am called to put to death every day. But I've learned to confess these moments immediately as sin, and claim God's immediate forgiveness, as he has promised.

DAVID: Wait a minute, Amanda! You don't *choose* to have moments when you feel same-sex attraction, do you? So if these attractions are involuntary, then how can you hold yourself responsible for having them? No one, not even you yourself, can blame you for having them. And if you can't be blamed, it isn't sin, and your guilt is false guilt. No repentance required!

AMANDA: I beg to differ, Dave. The desire for something sinful is itself sinful. That seems as plain as day to me. How can it not be?

STEPHANIE: It looks like we have on the table a number of issues we'll have to explore in greater detail later. First, there's the issue of having a gay "identity." Then there's the one about whether reparative therapy is effective or even a good thing. It is considered bad, even dangerous, not only by most non-Christians but also by many Christians. Third, there's the question of whether same-sex attraction, apart from same-sex behavior, is in itself sinful, so that if it is, same-sex attracted people need to continually repent and confess their moments of feeling same-sex attraction as sin. Okay, Amanda. Are you finished with your story or is there more?

AMANDA: There's more. A couple of years ago a Christian young man named Mike showed an interest in me. He was kind and considerate and I liked him a lot, but I wasn't in the least emotionally attracted to him. We did have some fun times together. After a while I noticed that he was beginning to develop feelings for me. This disturbed me a lot. When he told me about his feelings I was terrified. Should I tell him that his feelings weren't reciprocated and just end our relationship? Should I tell him that I want to be just friends and continue the relationship on that basis? Or should I tell him the truth, letting him know that I'm attracted to women and will never be attracted to any man? I went back and forth among these options. I didn't want to hurt him. I did enjoy his company. I prayed about it and felt the Lord telling me to be both vulnerable and truthful with Mike. Being truthful was the only option that would honor God. Mike might reject me, feeling shame and resentment that he had kept company with a same-sex attracted woman, and walk straight out of my life, but that was a risk I had to take. So one night, in a restaurant after we'd seen a movie, I looked him straight in the eye and told him. Tears welled up in his eyes and rolled down his cheeks. "I haven't told you this yet, but I'm in love with you, Amanda." His voice was choking. "You're the woman of my dreams. I can't imagine my life without you." Now it was my turn to cry. "Dear Mike," I said, "this can never be." It broke my heart to see him so sad. I did not see Mike for several weeks after that, and I did miss his company. I assumed that he had decided to end it, but one day he popped back into my life with a little square velvet box in his hand. Oh no! "Amanda," he said, "I've thought about it, I've prayed about it, and I've decided. I want you to marry me. I don't care that you're not sexually attracted to me. We don't have to have sex. All I want is to be with you every day, to care for you, to 'cherish' you—to hold you in my arms, even if you can't respond to me. The Bible doesn't forbid this type of marriage. Nowhere in the Bible does it say that you have to have sex to make a marriage." I burst into tears. "Dearest Mike," I sobbed, "I do love you as a friend. I do want you in my life. But what you're offering me is not something I can accept. I believe God designed sex to be a central part of marriage. A sexless marriage is a marriage in name only. I'm so afraid that at some point you'll crave sexual intimacy with me, and I won't be able to respond. That would be so overwhelmingly frustrating to us both. Yes, maybe this marriage would be within the biblical rules, but I doubt that it would be God-honoring." So, needless to say, the ring remained in the box. Mike has come back several times since, telling me repeatedly that he loves me and cannot imagine loving anyone else. One time he brought up the idea of us having children. That triggered a lot of emotions in me. Negative emotions—having children with him would involve sex with him, a thought that totally turned me off. But also positive emotions—I love children and have always wanted children of my own. Sarah and I had agreed that once we were married we would adopt. So I am torn. I haven't ended the relationship with Mike, but I haven't accepted his proposal either. I don't know what to do.

DAVID: You know, Amanda, there are a lot of "mixed orientation" marriages that seem to work out well. And, as your friend Mike pointed out, there are no biblical commands against it. A mixed orientation marriage is still a marriage between two people of opposite sexes. As for the sex thing, as long as your husband and you agree on how to navigate that, you are free to do as you like. Just remember that you're both called to submit to and sacrifice for each other. God will bless that.

AMANDA: Well, maybe I could learn to tolerate "the sex thing."

PHILIP: Whoa! I so disagree with you, Dave. There may not be a biblical command against a sexless marriage, but as Amanda herself suggested, a sexless marriage is a marriage in name only. There's more to biblical marriage than "staying within the biblical rules." Tolerate "the sex thing," Amanda? Is that what you believe is God's best for you? For a gay woman like you to marry and have sex with a straight man is totally unnatural! And imagine you and me getting married. That would be *doubly* unnatural, even if such a marriage is "within the rules!"

DAVID and AMANDA (together): Unnatural??

PHILIP: Yes, unnatural! Contrary to the way God created you, Amanda. God created you to be sexually attracted to women, not to men. For you to put yourself into a situation where, in order to have children, you have to force yourself to have sex with someone you're not naturally attracted to is to reject the way God created you. I won't go so far as to call that sin, but it does seem unhealthy at best and a road to relationship disaster at worst.

AMANDA: You're saying that God actually created me to be—in your words—"gay"?

PHILIP: That's exactly what I'm saying. I realize that this may sound like blasphemy to your ears, but I believe it to be true and defensible from the Bible.

DAVID: Now *that's* something I haven't heard before. I'd like to hear you make a case for that!

STEPHANIE: Well, for now let's add this as a fourth item to our list of issues to explore, whether people are gay because God created them that way. And a fifth is whether heterosexual sex between a straight person and a gay person is "unnatural" for the gay person. But if Amanda is finished telling her story, we'll go on with her "case" for the position she takes on our subject. Amanda?

AMANDA: Yes, I'm finished now. So I'll begin with the beginning, with three passages from the first two chapters of Genesis. Here they are:

First, Genesis 1:27:

> So God created man in his own image,
>   in the image of God he created him;
>   *male and female he created them.*

Second, Genesis 2:18:

> Then the Lord God said, "It is not good that the man should be alone; I will make him a *helper fit for* him."

And third, Genesis 2:20–24:

> But for Adam there was not found a *helper fit* for him. So the Lord God caused a deep sleep to fall upon *the man*, and while he slept took one of his ribs and closed up its place with flesh. And the rib that the Lord God had taken from the man he made into *a woman* and brought her to *the man*. Then the man said,
>
> > "This at last is bone of my bones
> >   and flesh of my flesh;
> > she shall be called Woman,
> >   because she was taken out of Man."
>
> Therefore *a man* shall leave his father and his mother and hold fast to *his wife*, and they shall become one flesh.

At this point I'd also like to add a New Testament text. It comes from Matthew's account of Jesus's teaching on marriage and divorce in chapter 19:4–5.

> [Jesus] answered, "Have you not read that he who created them from the beginning made them *male and female*, and said, 'Therefore *a man* shall leave his father and his mother and hold fast to *his wife*, and the two shall become one flesh'?"

So the Genesis account has God creating two and only two sexes, male and female. Since that creation links the two sexes to the creation of humankind in the image of God, we should probably conclude that being created in two sexes is in some way sacred because it reflects the very nature of God. And although the passage does not explicitly mention sexual desire, it is safe to assume that the male is created with built-in sexual desire for the female, and the female for the male. This rules out any homosexual desire as being proper to the creation of human beings. Such desire, let alone such behavior, is not in accordance with God's original design for human beings, and so is contrary to his will. And if it is contrary to his will, it is sin.

The second and third Genesis passages I cited concern God's design for the relationship between the male and the female. Genesis 2:18 reports the need for a "helper fit for" the man, and God's intention to provide for that need. I'm told that the original Hebrew phrase for "helper fit for . . ." is *ezer kenegdo*. There is debate about just what *ezer* ("helper") means in this context, but I want to focus on the other word, *kenegdo*. I'm told that it means "corresponding to [him]," or something like that: similar to, yet different from the man—someone who comes alongside (*ezer*) and is a counterpoint, or complement to him (*kenegdo*). None of the animals qualify as *kenegdo*; animals are too different. Yet the creation of another man would not be different enough (let alone the fact that it couldn't allow procreation to take place).

The third passage speaks of the union of male and female in a "one flesh" relationship. The expression refers to sexual union, and so it is a reference to marriage. So the teaching of the passage is that the marriage relationship is designed to be between a male and a female. And we find confirmation in Jesus's teaching in Matthew 19 that I also quoted. There Jesus frames his teaching about marriage by invoking the Genesis passages about the creation of humans as "male and female" as the prerequisite for the "one flesh" union that is marriage. This pretty definitively rules out same-sex marriage as being part of God's design. And, as I said, whatever violates God's design is against God's will and therefore sin.

So let me pause here for now. After a discussion of these passages, I'll turn to other texts in both the Old and the New Testament that explicitly condemn homosexuality as sin. I'll conclude with the New Testament teaching on the husband-wife relationship.

PHILIP: Good job so far, Amanda! You haven't said anything I haven't heard before, but you've said it with a lot more grace and clarity, let alone calm, than I usually hear it said. As a gay male Christian, this account of the Genesis passages is usually "preached" at me with index finger raised in a spirit of warning or judgment. And the passages you're going to discuss momentarily—the ones that condemn "homosexuality" (your term) explicitly—are used to clobber gay people in a way that is unbecoming to followers of Christ. I've experienced my share of pain at the hands of such brothers and sisters in Christ. That said, I do have a couple of questions about your account of God's "design."

AMANDA: Okay, shoot.

PHILIP: First a relatively minor one and then a weightier one. You said that the creation of human beings as male and female is an expression of the "image of God" in human beings. I know that theologians like Karl Barth have said that, but I'm not sure that that's correct. So I must ask, what is it in the nature of God that is imaged by the duality of male and female in humans?

AMANDA: I'm not sure I understand what you're getting at.

PHILIP: There is debate about exactly what it means for human beings to be created in the image of God. Based on a traditional understanding still widely accepted, when it is said that human beings uniquely bear the image of God (as animals don't), it means that human beings have a set of characteristics secondarily that God has primarily. So among God's creatures humans uniquely have the capacity to reason, to love, to communicate in language, to have a sense of right and wrong, and so on. We say that these are aspects of the "image of God" in humans because God has all of these capacities in a primary or original sense, and humans have them in a derived sense, just as an image of something displays derivatively various characteristics of the thing it reflects. So my question is, what is it in the nature of God of which the creation of humans in the duality of male and female is a derived expression? Does God express a duality of "male and female" in a primary, underived sense?

AMANDA: As I understand the nature of God, God is neither male nor female. Or perhaps I should say that God is both male and female. I'm not sure.

PHILIP: And secondly, not only are human beings created male and female, but animals are as well. But isn't the "image of God" designation applicable uniquely to human beings?

AMANDA: You're right. I don't think I really understand this. Perhaps being created in the image of God and being created male and female are two unconnected aspects of God's creation of humanity.

PHILIP: They are two distinct assertions, neither having any bearing on the other. The only reason I bring this up is that people often say homosexuality is sin because it does violence to the image of God in human beings. Gay people and transgender people as well are accused of perversely rejecting the image of God in which they are created. It is an unfounded accusation that hurts us deeply.

AMANDA: I'm sorry, Phil. I take back that part of what I said. But you said you had another, more weighty question.

PHILIP: Yes. If God's creation of humanity is as male and female and *only* as male and female, how do we account for the existence of intersex people? Some people are created neither exclusively male nor exclusively female. They have the chromosomal characteristics of both sexes. Sometimes at birth their genitalia are ambiguous, and parents are put in the impossible position of having to decide whether this baby is, or will be raised as, a boy or a girl. Doesn't the birth of such babies call into question the "binary" nature of God's design for humanity?

AMANDA: I'm familiar with this problem, but I'm not sure how to respond to it. I'll look into it. All I can say at this point is that this is a result of the fall of humanity, which occurred when Adam and Eve succumbed to the serpent's temptation and rebelled against God. That fall brought disastrous consequences upon God's perfect creation.

PHILIP: I'll accept this answer for now, but I think we will have to dig deeper at some later point. The issues of God's design for gender and sexuality, the role of the fall, and the manifest multiple sexual identities that we actually find in our world need to be examined both in light of the Bible and in light of our actual experience.

STEPHANIE: That may be an issue that you will want to take up when it's your turn, Phil. How about you, Dave? Do you have any questions for Amanda so far?

DAVID: As I said a moment ago, I'll defer my question about Amanda not wanting to identify herself as a gay person to later. As to her account of these Genesis passages, I'm in substantial agreement with her, so I have no questions for now. And I want to express to you, Phil, how sorry I am for the harsh and unloving ways this text and the "clobber" passages have been hurled at you and other gay men and women. That is not Jesus's way. I am glad, Amanda, that Pastor Kevin did not treat you that way. He is an example to the rest of us. I dare not think of what might have happened to you had you not had such a gracious and gentle counselor.

STEPHANIE: I don't have any questions for Amanda either at this point. The idea that these passages teach a divine "design" for human gender and sexuality is central to our topic and has far-reaching implications. I want to share some of my own thoughts on that idea when my turn comes up. Are you ready to go on, Amanda?

AMANDA: Yes. Let me begin by mentioning two passages in the Old Testament that are frequently brought up in the debate about homosexuality in the Bible, to get them out of the way. I think they are simply irrelevant. These passages are parts of stories that involve homosexual gang rape. The first is found in Genesis 19, in the story of Lot's angelic visitors in the city of Sodom. The second is found in Judges 19, as part of a bizarre story of homosexual (and heterosexual) violence. I won't waste any time on these stories. I'm sure all of us deplore sexual violence of any sort. In any case, the "sin" that Sodom is accused of elsewhere in the Bible (Ezekiel 16:49, for example) is not homosexuality—despite the currency of the English term "sodomy"—but lack of compassion for the poor and needy.

There are only two passages in the entire Old Testament that speak clearly and decisively to the issue of homosexuality. They both occur in the book of Leviticus and are part of the law given by God to Israel: Leviticus 18:22 and 20:13:

> You shall not *lie with a male as with a woman*; it is an abomination.

and

> If *a man lies with a male as with a woman*, both of them have committed an abomination; they shall surely be put to death; their blood is upon them.

In both texts male homosexual activity is condemned as "an abomination." In addition, the second text imposes the death penalty on both men involved in the act. And although female homosexual activity is not explicitly mentioned, these two verses are most naturally interpreted to cover that as well. "Abomination" is a strong word, in Hebrew as well as in English. The condemnation is unequivocal. And it is not hard to figure out why it is an abomination: for a man to have sexual intercourse with another man transgresses the principle of the distinctness of the sexes that was laid down in creation as stated in the first Genesis passage I discussed earlier. So Scripture accords with Scripture.

PHILIP: What strikes me as you expound on the meaning of these texts is that you supply an interpretation that you pull into the text, instead of drawing it out of the text. Theologians call this *eisegesis*, as opposed to *exegesis*, which is drawing out the meaning implicit in the text.

AMANDA: What do you mean?

PHILIP: All these texts say is that male same-sex behavior is offensive to God and that it is a capital crime. The texts say nothing about *why* the behavior is offensive to God. So when you say that the reason is that the behavior "transgresses the principle of the distinctness of the sexes that was laid down in creation," you are speculating. It may well be offensive to God for some other reason.

AMANDA: But as long as the behavior is offensive to God, whatever God's reason may be, isn't that enough to regard it as sin and therefore to be avoided?

PHILIP: There may be a cultural reason—a reason that applied at that time but no longer applies today—that explains God's displeasure with the act.

STEPHANIE: Perhaps you could say more about that when it's your turn next week, Phil. For now I think we should let Amanda go on.

AMANDA: Okay. When we turn to the New Testament, we find a couple of passages in which homosexuality is included in "vice lists"—lists of sinful behaviors that exclude people from the kingdom of God. Here are the two passages.

1 Corinthians 6:9–11:

> Or do you not know that the unrighteous will not inherit the king-dom of God? Do not be deceived: neither the sexually immoral, nor idolaters, nor adulterers, nor *men who practice homosexual-ity*, nor thieves, nor the greedy, nor drunkards, nor revilers, nor swindlers will inherit the kingdom of God. And such were some of you. But you were washed, you were sanctified, you were justified in the name of the Lord Jesus Christ and by the Spirit of our God.

1 Timothy 1:8–11:

> Now we know that the law is good, if one uses it lawfully, under-standing this, that the law is not laid down for the just but for the lawless and disobedient, for the ungodly and sinners, for the unholy and profane, for those who strike their fathers and moth-ers, for murderers, the sexually immoral, *men who practice homo-sexuality*, enslavers, liars, perjurers, and whatever else is contrary to sound doctrine, in accordance with the gospel of the glory of the blessed God with which I have been entrusted.

Notice how the phrase, "men who practice homosexuality," occurs in both of these lists. Again, although it is not explicit, women who practice homosexuality are probably included as well. The sanction against all the behaviors on these vice lists is that the people practicing them "will not inherit the kingdom of God." There is only one way out: to be "washed . . . sanctified . . . and justified in the name of the Lord Jesus Christ and by the Spirit of our God." Even though I am not a man, I can really identify with this passage. "And such was I." When I came to faith in Christ, God gave me the grace to abandon my lesbian lifestyle, and so I was "washed, sanctified, and justified," even though I am still waiting for release from my same-sex attraction. The implicit warning in these passages remains clear, however: as long as one continues to "practice homosexuality," one is "unrighteous" and cannot inherit the Kingdom of God—that is, one cannot be saved.

PHILIP: There is a translation issue with these texts, Amanda, that you seem to be unaware of. The phrase "men who practice homosexuality" is not really a translation of the Greek—it's more of a paraphrase. The terms "homosexual" and "homosexuality" are not found anywhere in the Bible.

These words are a nineteenth-century invention. And just about every modern English translation of the Bible resorts to a paraphrase instead of translating the original Greek words literally. By doing so they obscure the actual meaning of the text. I promise to talk about that next week, so I won't press the point now.

AMANDA: All right, I'll go on then. Let me turn to the Bible's clearest, longest, and most forceful condemnation of homosexuality. This comes in the first chapter of Paul's letter to the Romans. I'll quote the passage in full.

Romans 1:18–27:

> For the wrath of God is revealed from heaven against all ungodliness and unrighteousness of men, who by their unrighteousness suppress the truth. For what can be known about God is plain to them, because God has shown it to them. For his invisible attributes, namely, his eternal power and divine nature, have been clearly perceived, ever since the creation of the world, in the things that have been made. So they are without excuse. For although they knew God, they did not honor him as God or give thanks to him, but they became futile in their thinking, and their foolish hearts were darkened. Claiming to be wise, they became fools, and exchanged the glory of the immortal God for images resembling mortal man and birds and animals and creeping things. Therefore God gave them up in the *lusts of their hearts* to *impurity*, to the *dishonoring of their bodies among themselves*, because they exchanged the truth about God for a lie and worshiped and served the creature rather than the Creator, who is blessed forever! Amen. For this reason God gave them up to *dishonorable passions*. For their *women exchanged natural relations for those that are contrary to nature*; and the *men likewise gave up natural relations with women* and were *consumed with passion for one another, men committing shameless acts with men* and receiving in themselves the due penalty for their error.

In this passage Paul makes a powerful and effective argument to the effect that homosexuality, along with a list of other sins that he goes on to mention in verses 28–32, is the consequence of humanity's universal rebellion against God. All human beings, he argues first, have an innate knowledge of God, revealed to them through creation. That revelation in creation is sufficient to establish their knowledge of God's "eternal power and divine nature"—that is, of God's authority over their lives and their duty to worship and obey God. So they are held accountable to that revelation; they are "without excuse." Second, all human beings have chosen to suppress that knowledge, exchanging the truth about God for a lie, and instead of worshiping the true God, they direct their impulse to worship away from the true God, their Creator, and toward created objects, idols. This is no doubt a reference to the fall of Genesis 3 and its aftermath. Third, this deliberate "darkening" in their hearts led God to "give them up," abandoning them to their own devices. So, left to their own devices, their religious perversity expressed itself in moral perversity and depravity. The clearest and most graphic manifestation of their moral depravity, though not the only one, is homosexuality. Listen to the phrases that describe their predicament, the "lusts of their hearts," their "impurity," their "dishonoring of their bodies among themselves," their giving themselves over to "dishonorable passions," their women "exchanging natural relations for those that are contrary to nature," their men "consumed with passion for one another, committing shameless acts with men." Paul's language is uncompromising and sweeping. His denunciation of homosexuality as "contrary to nature" is at the heart of his condemnation. There is nothing at all in the passage to suggest that there are exceptions, that certain kinds of homosexual acts and passions are okay while others are not. To try to find such exceptions and exclude them from the universality of Paul's condemnation is a hopeless attempt to excuse the inexcusable.

PHILIP: There is no doubt that Paul's language is sweeping and uncompromising. But here's a problem for me. You say the description is universal. You've used the phrase, "all human beings," twice, and the words "universal" and "universality" as well. You've attributed this condition to the fall, which, I agree, is indeed universal in its scope. But you're not suggesting that *all* fallen human beings are same-sex attracted, are you? Because that's clearly false.

AMANDA: I agree that that's false. While the fall was universal, this particular effect of the fall is not. *All* people are fallen, but only *some* people engage in same-sex behavior and have same-sex desires.

PHILIP: Then what explains the fact that *some* people engage in this disgusting behavior and have these disgusting desires and passions, but not others?

AMANDA: It's because these people *choose* to "exchange" their natural (I suppose that means heterosexual) dispositions for unnatural (homosexual) ones, and act on those dispositions, while others do not. Even though they are fallen, they still have free will.

PHILIP: Did *you* choose to "exchange" a supposedly "natural" heterosexual disposition for your same-sex one? Did you *choose* to become gay, Amanda—excuse me, same-sex attracted?

AMANDA: No, I didn't.

PHILIP: Neither did I. So can you see *yourself* in this picture, Amanda? I'm not being difficult. I really want to know.

AMANDA: Well, I didn't choose to *become* same-sex attracted. I would describe myself as always having been that way. I still am. And since I didn't believe in God until recently I can't say that I consciously rebelled against God—that I "exchanged" the truth of God that I somehow already knew for a lie. It would be truer to say that I was born and raised in a lie about God and when I became a Christian I "exchanged" that lie for the truth about God.

PHILIP: Well said, Amanda. This is what really troubles me. So many people who take your view of this passage tell me that I'm not just a fallen human being like everybody else, but I'm doubly fallen because I've chosen to compound my fallenness by "exchanging" my supposed natural heterosexuality for a perverse unnatural homosexuality.

DAVID: Wait, Phil. You're trying to see how your or Amanda's personal history fits into the passage. Maybe that's the wrong approach. Maybe we should read the passage more generally. What if it is saying that homosexuality is a *collective* consequence of the fall, that left to its own devices humanity has cast off the restraint that the worship of the true God would have left in place? Such lack of restraint would be manifest in the way *some*, but not necessarily *all*, humans have decided to live.

PHILIP: I have a problem with that, Dave. But I'll wait until another time to state what that is. Amanda, you said that you also wanted to look at a New Testament passage that speaks to the spousal relationship in marriage. Why don't you go on to that passage?

AMANDA: Okay, here's the passage.

Ephesians 5:22–32:

> Wives, submit to your own husbands, as to the Lord. For the husband is the head of the wife even as Christ is the head of the church, his body, and is himself its Savior. Now as the church submits to Christ, so also wives should submit in everything to their husbands. Husbands, love your wives, as Christ loved the church and gave himself up for her, that he might sanctify her, having cleansed her by the washing of water with the word, so that he might present the church to himself in splendor, without spot or wrinkle or any such thing, that she might be holy and without blemish. In the same way husbands should love their wives as their own bodies. He who loves his wife loves himself. For no one ever hated his own flesh, but nourishes and cherishes it, just as Christ does the church, because we are members of his body. "Therefore a man shall leave his father and mother and hold fast to his wife, and the two shall become one flesh." This mystery is profound, and I am saying that it refers to Christ and the church.

I don't want to focus so much on the issue that is more frequently debated about this passage, which is whether it teaches that a wife is in some sense subordinate to her husband. Instead I want to examine the analogy Paul draws between the husband-wife relationship and the Christ-church relationship. As Christ is the head of his church, Paul says, so a husband is the head of his wife. And conversely, as the church is the body of Christ, so a wife is the body of her husband (this is certainly implied even if not explicitly stated). But how does this head-body relationship play out in a same-sex marriage? Same-sex marriages have either two husbands or two wives. These marriages don't display the organic union of head and body. Neither two bodiless heads nor two headless bodies make a marriage. How can the "mystery" of Christ's relationship to the church be reflected in marriages that do not include the distinction between husband and wife, and so between male and female? We may *call* a same-sex marriage "marriage," but is it really so, if the differentiation that corresponds to that between Christ and the church cannot be displayed within it?

So let me conclude by summing up my position. First, I affirm, as the church has historically done, that God created humanity as male and female, and that this binary creation is God's design or intent for human gender and sexuality. God created males to be sexually attracted to females, and females to males, so sexual attraction and behavior between two males or between two females violates God's creation order and is contrary to God's intent. Whatever is contrary to God's intent is sin, so homosexual attraction and behavior is sin for just that reason. The Bible is consistent in its condemnation of such attraction and behavior. It follows from this that same-sex relationships, whether "married" or not, are sinful and to be forbidden. Homosexual sin, both the desire and the behavior, should be repented of and confessed. God will forgive all sin that is sincerely repented of and confessed, and homosexual sin is no exception. The options open to people like myself who persist in experiencing same-sex attractions are, first, to disavow and avoid same-sex behavior in all of its forms. Second, to confess to God any flare-ups of same-sex attraction as they occur. Third, to seek help in reversing one's same-sex attractions; and fourth, if such help is not available or successful, either to commit to a celibate life or some form of heterosexual marriage.

I'm sorry, guys. I know each of you will have different thoughts about these passages than I do. Part of me wants to listen to you and hear your thoughts and allow my own thinking to be open to yours. But there's another part of me that remains convinced that the Bible is wholly clear and unequivocal in its condemnation of homosexuality for the reasons I've set out. As believers we are called to live our lives and pursue our relationships in conformity with God's design for our sexuality. That design allows for only one God-blessed expression of our sexuality: intimacy within heterosexual marriage. Otherwise we sin, from which we need to repent, receive forgiveness, and move on. I have lived this and am still living it personally. For me it is not easy, but it is right.

PHILIP: Before we let you go, Amanda, I just want to pick up on your use of the phrase, " . . . *violates* God's creation order." The verb "violates" suggests the idea that gay people, in an attitude of oppositional defiance, willfully transgress boundaries that God has put in place. Even saying that same-sex desire and behavior are "*contrary* to God's intent" suggests a measure of indifference to God's will on the part of gay people. This paints a very negative picture of our motivations that is neither accurate nor charitable. Why not use more neutral language, like "does not conform to" or "is not aligned with" God's creation order? This says all that you want or need to say and does not impute contrarian attitudes to gay folks. It is not uncommon among people who take your position on the issue to use emotionally laden language against gays and lesbians, which is totally unnecessary, inappropriate, and undeserved.

AMANDA: I take your point, Phil. I'll try to remember that. Please forgive me if I don't do that consistently.

STEPHANIE: Amanda, thanks for sharing your heart as well as your thoughts and how you see the Bible speaking to our topic. You have set the table for our coming conversations and have given us much to think about. You've already received some response, particularly from Phil and Dave, so I'm wondering if we shouldn't just call it a night.

PHILIP: I just want to thank Amanda for her honesty and vulnerability tonight. I can understand how hard this must be for her. Next week I'll be presenting a very different take on the passages she outlined tonight, and I'll come to a different conclusion. But I want you to know, Amanda, that I respect you and will always be your friend.

AMANDA: Thanks Phil. I really do appreciate that.

Questions for Reflection and Discussion on Dialogue 1

1. What is your own experience with homosexuality? What stories about yourself, your family, or any of your friends would you be willing to share in a group setting?

2. What, if anything, strikes you about Amanda's story of her conversion? How do you respond to similar stories? Do you identify more with Amanda's account of her experience of God or with the questions about it raised by the other characters?

3. The idea of having a "gay identity" is controversial among Christians. Do you think that being same-sex attracted is or is not part of a person's "identity," that is, an essential aspect of that person and not just some incidental fact about them? Explain.

4. What do you think of the idea of a "mixed orientation" marriage? Would you be inclined to agree more with David, who approves of it, or with Philip, who disapproves of it? Why?

5. Do you agree with Amanda that the stories about homosexual rape in Genesis and Judges have no relevance to the Bible's teaching about homosexuality? If you disagree, explain.

6. What is your view of the fact that some individuals are born "intersex"? How do you fit that fact into the teaching (in Genesis 1:27) that God created human beings "male and female"?

7. Amanda lays out the traditional conservative case against homosexual behavior and homosexual relationships. Discuss the following components of that case:

- The "binary" nature of gender distinction in Genesis 1.

- Heterosexuality as a requirement for sexual relationships and marriage.

- The reason(s) for God's prohibition of sexual intercourse between males.

- Paul's strongly worded condemnation of homosexual passion and behavior in Romans 1.

8. What questions does Philip raise about Amanda's accounts of the texts she discusses (the Leviticus texts, the vice lists in the New Testament and Rom 1)? Are these valid questions, in your view?

9. Do you find Amanda's case for her views plausible and persuasive? What reservations, if any, do you have about it?

Dialogue 2

The four friends meet again the following Friday night.

STEPHANIE: It's great to see everyone tonight. I hope we've all had a good week. I'm sure all of us have midterms and due dates for papers coming up as the middle of the semester is fast approaching. I'm glad we're making these conversations a priority, though. Tonight is Phil's turn to tell his story and give his account of how he understands the biblical passages that speak to our issue. Are you ready, Phil?

PHILIP: I'm good to go. May I pray first? *All murmur agreement. Philip continues.*

> *Lord Jesus, here we are again, our hearts united in friendship, even if our viewpoints are diverse. Thank you for your love for me, which has not and will not let me go. We confess, Lord, that we are all broken, and that we all need your healing. Give me your grace as I tell my story tonight and help me—help all of us—to be humble, vulnerable, and teachable, as I present a case for my view. Let this not be just a theological debate but an opportunity to grow together in mutual understanding, love, and support. You know the longing of my heart, Lord, which is to be unconditionally accepted by my Christian friends, as I am by you, whatever theological positions we might hold on our subject. In your name, Lord, Amen.*

So let me begin with my story. I grew up in a very conservative Christian home, the second of four children. Our family was part of a close-knit church-centered community. The pastor was the spiritual head of our church; and on matters of belief and conduct, as well as on what was or wasn't allowed in the church, he was the sole and unquestioned authority. Everyone in our church, my parents included, deferred to his authority.

When I was about five years old, my mother prayed with me to accept Jesus as my Savior. I faithfully attended Sunday school and soaked up numerous Bible stories and their application to my life. Several years later I began attending "big church" with my parents and older sister. Singing the old hymns moved me deeply. I quickly and effortlessly internalized the lyrics and the tunes. I found myself singing the verses in harmony, even though at that time I could not read music yet. I strongly sensed God revealing his truth, his beauty, and especially his love to me, and this created in me a deep longing to worship God and give my whole life over to him in praise. I made up my mind that I wanted to study music and prepare myself for a career as a minister of music in a church setting. My parents bought a piano and hooked me up with a first-rate music teacher to begin piano lessons.

I was a quick study, and within a very short time became a pretty proficient pianist. I began to play hymn arrangements and improvisations as "special music" occasionally at church services. At the age of 12 I was invited to become one of the regular accompanists on both the organ and the piano for congregational singing. Congregational response was overwhelmingly affirming! I loved this! God had given me a gift, I was good at what I did, and I loved using my gift for God's glory.

As I grew into puberty, I became aware of a sexual attraction to other boys. I developed a crush on one particular boy who I was sure would reciprocate. Instead, he was repelled. I was crushed. The word got out: "Phil is *gay*." Is it true, I asked myself? Am I really gay? I had not experienced any attraction to girls. No flutter of the heart, no dryness in the mouth. From our pastor's occasional mentions of "homosexuality" in his sermons, I knew that being gay was very wrong, and I had no reason to question the assertion that it is condemned in the Bible. Every night I would pray long and hard that I would not be gay. I longed for any hopeful sign that I would be attracted to girls. But no such sign ever came.

I lived in fear for a long time. What if I really am gay? Had word gotten out to my parents? Would they still love me? What if the pastor had got wind of it? What would happen to me in church? Would I be dismissed from my piano playing? Would I be kicked out of the church? And if so, what would happen to my dream career as music minister?

In my turmoil I went to a place where many of us who struggle with these doubts go—the Internet. *Am I going through a stage, or is this permanent? If I really am gay, can I be "fixed"?* Above all, *will God still love me if I am gay?* It didn't take long to discover that there were many others who were or had been in the exact same place that I was. So I entered into chat rooms with others, all of us anonymous, all of us sharing our experiences. The stories were diverse: "My parents kicked me out of the house when I came out to them." "My parents stood with me, but my church was another story." "I couldn't bear the agony. I began to hate myself and tried to commit suicide." Even, "I don't believe anymore. I'm done with church and Christianity."

Many chat partners gave me advice about coming out, but much of it was contradictory and not very helpful. Eventually I decided to come out to my parents; it was the honest thing to do, and I mentally prepared myself for every possible reaction. The three of us sat in the living room, and I said the words, "Mom and Dad, I need to tell you something. I'm gay." That was all. My parents sat in stunned silence. Mom began to cry. After a minute or so, my dad got up from his seat and said, "Thanks for telling us, Phil. This must have been really hard for you." He hugged me, and we both broke down in tears. Mom joined our hug, and we all cried together. Although this was incredibly sad I felt a huge sense of relief.

Afterwards my dad told me that he had heard rumors but decided to put no stock in them. After all, he told me, adolescent sexuality is fluid, and a rumor is just a rumor. He told me that he hadn't noticed anything in my behavior to confirm the rumors. He also told me that he loved me: "always have, always will." He, Mom, and I would figure this out together.

We agreed that the three of us together would tell our pastor, and so we requested a meeting with him. The pastor's face went rigid when I again uttered the words, "I am gay." "This affects not only you and your parents," he began, "but the entire church. 1 Corinthians 5:6 says, 'Know ye not that a little leaven leaveneth the whole lump?' As the pastor of this church I am called to 'purge out the old leaven.' The Bible is clear: homosexuality is sin. In the very next chapter the Bible specifically excludes homosexuals from inheriting the kingdom of God. I must therefore ask you, Phil, to separate yourself from our church. For your sake we'll try to keep this as quiet as we can."

That was the end of the conversation. I was crushed. On the way home, Mom and Dad told me that they also could not stay at the church. Mom cried again. We never went back.

I have not succeeded in finding a church that fully, and without qualification, accepts gays and lesbians and also preaches the gospel of salvation in Christ alone. Those churches that would accept me have, in my opinion, a much too weak and deficient view of Scripture and of Christ, while those who have a strong gospel message and witness always accept us, if they do at all, with some qualification or other. I am welcome to their fellowship, but there are exclusions—from membership, for example, or from leadership, or from preaching or teaching, and so on. I've had to put aside my dream of a career as minister of music. The churches that would have me I don't particularly want to be part of, while the churches that I would love to be part of won't hire a gay music minister. So I'll be doing graduate work in the field of Religious Studies and some day hope to teach at an institution where my being gay is not an issue. Maybe I could take a side job as minister of music in a gospel-centered church that doesn't object to having a gay minister of music on its staff, if there even is such a church.

DAVID: Don't hold your breath, Phil.

PHILIP: I'm not. I can still hope, though. Anyhow, there's more to my story that you may or may not want to know. A few years ago I met another gay Christian young man online. We began to correspond and discovered many mutual interests. His name is James, and he is an amazing artist. He sent me some photographs of his art. We were thrilled to discover that many of our other passions are similar. We both love the outdoors, camping, hiking, and mountain climbing. James plays guitar really well, and with my piano skills we could see ourselves making great music together. We both like cooking and entertaining friends. Above all, like me, James loves Jesus. We were drawn to each other. After a couple of months we arranged to meet. I traveled to his home, close to the mountains, and we hiked one of the famous trails there together. We played music together. Being together brought such joy to us. James has also visited me at my home. Our friendship evolved into romantic attraction and we fell in love. Not long after we realized this we both sensed the need for a time-out period to discern whether the Lord was truly in our relationship. We wanted above all for Christ to be the center of our lives and could not imagine going forward without his blessing. Would God permit us to get married, and all that that entails, including starting a sexual relationship? As Christians both of us are virgins, and both of us believe strongly that sex is for marriage only. Even so, given the almost universal consensus against same-sex marriage in the conservative Christian communities in which we were raised, we wanted to be extremely cautious. We studied the very Bible passages that Amanda laid out for us last week, read a lot of books on both sides of this issue, and sought counsel from other believers. Eventually we came to the conclusion that when the Bible speaks so strongly against homosexuality—and there's no doubt that it does—it addresses the numerous perverted homosexual practices of the surrounding pagan nations in the Middle Eastern and later in the Greek and Roman cultures of the day. Faithful, monogamous, and lifelong homosexual relationships were all but unknown in biblical times; and even if they were, they were not the object of condemnation in either testament. And Jesus never even mentions homosexuality in the Gospels. It doesn't appear to be an issue for him. Our study, bathed in prayer, brought us to a place of peace and a sense of God's affirmation of our intentions. We plan to be married in June after I graduate. So that's my story. Do any of you have a comment or a question for me?

AMANDA: Thanks for your story, Phil. Similar to mine, yet so very different. We are similar in that both of us are same-sex attracted. But we're different in that I struggle against my attractions, but you seem to have accepted yours. We're also different in that I've had a considerable number of same-sex experiences in high school, while you're a virgin. That blows my preconception of people who call themselves gay. I had automatically assumed that anyone who identified as gay and was not committed to lifelong celibacy—as clearly you are not—would also have had a lot of same-sex experiences in their history. Being gay and holding to a traditional "no sex until marriage" ethic seemed so contradictory to me that I never gave a thought to the situation that you and James represent. Even so, you know from my talk last week that I do not agree that your "marriage" to James is God's way for you.

PHILIP: I do know that, Amanda, and I don't expect that my story will have changed your mind. But I hope you also realize that our decision to get married wasn't made without doing our due spiritual diligence. As to our being virgins, I guess James and I are breaking a stereotype that has long been hurtful to us. When people hear I'm gay, they almost always assume I'm sexually active. I've heard through the grapevine that a number of Christian people who know me and know about our forthcoming marriage assume that James and I are already having sex when they wouldn't necessarily assume that about a straight Christian couple.

DAVID: That is sad, Phil. We're all guilty of putting people in one box or another. This prevents us from getting to know other people as real people. I am aware that gay and lesbian folks are especially vulnerable to that, especially by straight Christians. We put a label on people and then see them as "the other," a population to be feared and resisted, instead of the individual people they are, to be reached out to and loved as they are—as Christ reached out to and loved all of us as we were.

That said, Phil, like Amanda I am very skeptical about whether the Bible permits same-sex marriage, and thus that your forthcoming marriage to James has God's blessing. Let's just say that I need to be convinced that there is a solid biblical case to be made. I'm open to being convinced, but I need you to know that I'm no pushover.

PHILIP: I'll accept that as a challenge. I'll do my best to convince you.

STEPHANIE: Thank you, Phil. Are you ready to get into the Bible passages and explain how you interpret them?

PHILIP: Yes. I'd like to start with the Genesis passage Amanda began with, only I'd like to set it in the context of the creation account that preceded it. I'm sure all of us are familiar, at least in outline, with that account. The account begins with Day 1: the creation of light and the separation of that light from darkness, and God's calling the light "day," and the darkness "night." So there is separation and duality. But of course between day and night there are also the transitional stages between light and darkness, between "day" and "night," namely dawn and dusk. These are left unmentioned in the account. But that does not mean, of course, that dawn and dusk were not included in the creation of day and night. On Day 2 there is again separation and duality: the waters above the expanse are separated from the waters below the expanse. But that does not mean that there is never any mist or fog between the upper and lower realms of water. On Day 3 we have within the lower realm of water a separation of sea from dry land. Again, separation and duality. But what about marshes and estuaries? These are "in between" areas that are neither exclusively sea nor exclusively land. Here, too, we should not assume that just because they are not mentioned, they are excluded from creation. Then later, still on Day 3, God again creates a duality: plants bearing seeds and trees bearing fruit. But the account itself acknowledges that this duality is somewhat artificial: the

35

fruit of trees is their seed, so trees are actually seed-bearing plants as well. Nevertheless they are distinguished because the structure of the account in terms of separation and duality seems to require it. On Day 4 we again have separation and duality: the sun as the light for the day and the moon as the light for the night (the stars are thrown in as an afterthought). On Day 5, we are given the creation of the duality of aquatic animals and animals that fly in the air. No mention of animals that are at home both in the water and the sky, like pelicans. And on Day 6 land animals are created. But what about amphibians like frogs and salamanders? Where do they fit? Are they aquatic animals, created on Day 5, or land animals, created on Day 6?

So what's my point? It is this. The creation account of Genesis 1 neither is nor is meant to be an exhaustive account of all the varieties of things that God creates. The groupings are broad and general. There are creatures that do not fit neatly into a particular classification. And the account is driven by duality, the distinctions between opposites.

Let me remind us of the question I asked Amanda last week, and put it in the context I've just provided. On Day 6 God creates human beings, in the duality of male and female. This duality, I want to say, is the culmination of the progression of the dualities in the accounts of the previous creation days. But this duality completely overlooks the existence of people who are intersex, neither distinctly male nor distinctly female. In that way intersex people are like dawn and dusk, marshes and estuaries, frogs and salamanders. But they are nevertheless among God's creatures, not imports from some alien world. And all that God creates is good. So, I have to take exception to Amanda's tentative explanation that they are somehow the results of the fall. Are dawn and dusk, marshes and estuaries, and frogs and salamanders also "the result of the fall"? That seems absurd.

My broader point is this. If God creates not only males and females but also intersex people, and if we find in our world not only straight people but also gay folks like Amanda and myself, as well as people who are transgender—who have come to identify as one gender when their anatomical sex is of the other—then we should seriously question whether God's design of humanity as "binary," exclusively male and female, with only heterosexual attraction for each other, represents the fullness of creation that we actually find. Such a binary design, I suggest, is a Platonic fiction: a heavenly ideal world that does not correspond to the earthly reality we actually experience. The world of humanity that God actually creates does indeed contain a majority of cisgender heterosexual males and females, just as it contains a majority of right-handed people. But it also contains a minority of people of other genders and sexual identities, just as it contains a minority of left-handed people. Left-handedness isn't a result of the fall. Left-handed people are not broken, and they don't need fixing. Gay people are not broken and don't need fixing. The results of reparative therapy have been at best unsuccessful and at worst disastrous. Besides, people of minority sexual identities add diversity and variety to our world, just as the many and various people of diverse ethnicities and skin colors do. They enrich our interactions with one another, opening us up to other experiences, other histories and other ways of seeing the world. It makes me tremendously sad to see so many of my fellow Christians isolate themselves from these interactions because of their impoverished understanding of the richness and diversity of God's creation.

DAVID: Well said, Phil. You won't be surprised when I tell you that I don't agree with you, but you've made your point very effectively. And, as an aside, you've cast aspersions on one of my favorite philosophers, Plato. Ouch! I'll reserve my critique of your view of God's design in creation in Genesis 1 when my turn comes next week.

PHILIP: I did indeed suspect that you wouldn't agree with me, Dave. Sorry about Plato. I guess I'm more of an Aristotelian, more oriented to the world that actually is than to an unattainable ideal world. By the way, we haven't heard much from Stephanie on any of this. She seems to be holding her cards pretty close to her vest.

STEPHANIE: I can't overstate the importance of the point at issue. But if you don't mind, I'll hold onto my cards for a little while longer. Why don't we ask Phil to give us his take on the other biblical passages, the Leviticus texts and the New Testament passages?

AMANDA: Before Phil does that, shouldn't we ask him about his view of the passages in Genesis 2, about the need of a "fit helper" for Adam, and about the "one flesh" union between Adam and his fit helper?

PHILIP: If you don't mind, Amanda, I'd like to leave the question of same-sex marriage and my view of it based on those and other scriptures until after we've had a look at my take on the homosexuality texts. Is that okay? As to those texts, let me begin by stating my agreement with Amanda that the Old Testament passages relating the homosexual gang rapes of Genesis 19 and Judges 19 are "off the table." But I do want to say something about why I think these passages should play no part in our discussion.

DAVID: I'm also troubled by the frequent appeal to those passages in many discussions about what the Bible teaches about homosexuality, but I'd like to hear your take on it.

PHILIP: If we view these passages as having any negative implication about the morality of homosexual behavior per se, we'd have to say that, other things being equal, heterosexual gang rape is somehow morally preferable to homosexual gang rape. And we'd also have to say—again, other things being equal—that Lot's offer of his virgin daughters to the mob as replacements for his angelic visitors (Genesis 19:6–9) as more appropriate objects for the satisfaction of their violent impulses, is morally commendable. Does anyone want to say that?

DAVID: It's worth noting that neither the gang rape as such nor its homosexual aspect is condemned in the passage. The passage is pure narrative and includes no ethical or theological commentary on the attempted rape. This is of course not to say that the passage condones it, but it does bring up the difficulty of drawing ethical or theological teaching from passages that are purely narrative.

PHILIP: It's probably safe to assume that the narrator of the passage would condemn it, but the passage gives no *independent* evidence of the unacceptability of the behavior described, and so the passage should not be counted among those that provide any biblical teaching about the moral status of homosexuality. For that teaching we need to go to other passages. So, let's go to those other passages, beginning with the two verses in Leviticus, which I'll quote for us again.

Leviticus 18:22 and 20:13:

You shall not *lie with a male as with a woman*; it is an abomination.

If *a man lies with a male as with a woman*, both of them have committed an abomination; they shall surely be put to death; their blood is upon them.

It's important to see these texts as part of the larger whole in which they're found. They are found inside a section of Leviticus often referred to as the "Holiness Code" (Leviticus 17–26). The theme verse for this code is Leviticus 19:2, "You shall be holy, for I the Lord your God am holy." The commands and prohibitions in the Holiness Code are meant to set God's covenant people apart from the surrounding nations, particularly Egypt, the nation they have left, and Canaan, the nation God is calling them to possess (Leviticus 18:3). The call to live differently from the pagan nations creates the presumption that the forbidden practices dubbed "abominable" were rampant in those nations. These practices will have included various forms of homosexuality, perhaps associated with pagan rituals, or with prostitution, or forms of exploitation. There is evidence in the Bible itself that there was a practice of male shrine prostitution (see, for example, I Kings 14:24, 15:12) that the apostate kings of Judah introduced into the land. This practice must have come from somewhere.

DAVID: I think there may be a translation issue here, Phil. I read somewhere that recent scholarship has questioned the accepted translation of a certain Hebrew expression as "male shrine prostitutes," and that many scholars consequently deny the existence of such a practice in the Old Testament world.

STEPHANIE: The jury is still out on that, I believe. Whichever way it eventually goes, the point is well taken that we need to be extremely careful in making historical judgments based on controversial translations of the original texts.

PHILIP: All right, I won't press that point. Going back to the texts, there is also a suggestion that lying with a man "as with a woman" treats the man lain with in a degrading way. Treating a man as though he were a woman is demeaning that man, given that in that culture women were considered inferior to men. So the Levitical prohibition is most likely a prohibition that presupposes patriarchy. However we read this, it's worth noting that while this practice is described as an abomination, there is no explanation as to *why* it is abominable. As I mentioned last week, Amanda's suggestion that the abomination consists in the transgression of a God-designed boundary between the sexes is, in my humble opinion and with all due respect, purely speculative. That interpretation has to be read *into* the text. It cannot be elicited *out of* it. The many other practices described as abominable in these chapters do not always violate creation ordinances. Many, such as wearing garments made out of two different kinds of fabrics (Leviticus 19:19), are presumably cultural. No one is flouting a divine intention by wearing cotton-polyester clothing!

AMANDA: On the other hand, the prohibition of practices such as child sacrifice to Molech (Leviticus 18:21), clearly transcends cultural norms. I agree that these male homosexuality texts by themselves do not spell out the reason or reasons God has for declaring this activity to be abominable, so however you fill that gap would involve speculation, or *eisegesis*, as you called it last week. But that applies to your suggestion as well as to mine. What's sauce for the goose—

DAVID: —is sauce for the gander. So this means that we can't derive a definitive conclusion from these Leviticus texts either way. The prohibition *could* reflect a cultural situation no longer applicable today, but it also *could* express a universal moral principle applicable to all people at all times. We will have to turn to the New Testament passages to shed light on the correct interpretation and application of these texts.

PHILIP: So let's go there, beginning with the vice lists of 1 Corinthians 6 and 1 Timothy 1 that Amanda cited last week. As I briefly commented then, in the translation that she quoted from, the phrase "men who practice homosexuality" occurs in both passages. That phrase is more of a paraphrase than a translation. I should add that in most other contemporary English translations of the Bible, you'll find some paraphrase or other and not an actual translation here. In the first of these two passages the phrase actually refers to two distinct groups of men. A literal translation of the term used for the first group is "softies." The Greek term is *malakoi* (singular: *malakos*). And a literal translation of that for the second group is "male-bedders." The Greek term is *arsenokoitai* (singular: *arsenokoitēs*). In the latter passage, only the second of these two terms appears. So, using the literal translation instead of the paraphrase, the two texts read as follows:

1 Corinthians 6:9–11:

> Or do you not know that the unrighteous will not inherit the kingdom of God? Do not be deceived: neither the sexually immoral,

nor idolaters, nor adulterers, nor *softies*, nor *male-bedders*, nor
thieves, nor the greedy, nor drunkards, nor revilers, nor swindlers
will inherit the kingdom of God. And such were some of you.
But you were washed, you were sanctified, you were justified in
the name of the Lord Jesus Christ and by the Spirit of our God.

And 1 Timothy 1:8–11:

Now we know that the law is good, if one uses it lawfully, understanding this, that the law is not laid down for the just but for the
lawless and disobedient, for the ungodly and sinners, for the un-
holy and profane, for those who strike their fathers and mothers,
for murderers, the sexually immoral, *male-bedders*, enslavers, li-
ars, perjurers, and whatever else is contrary to sound doctrine, in
accordance with the gospel of the glory of the blessed God with
which I have been entrusted.

So here's my question: Who are these softies and male-bedders? Are
these, as Amanda's translation suggests, any men engaged in homosexual
acts, with the "receptive" man in the role of the softy, and the "penetrating"
man in the role of the male-bedder? Or are they a subset of them? The term
"softy" is vague. It doesn't refer exclusively to someone engaged in male homosexual intercourse. I have studied some of the scholarly literature on the
meanings of these two terms in these texts. I get the sense that both of these
terms are pejorative terms, possibly even vulgar. Several scholars suggest
that softies were probably male prostitutes, and male-bedders the clients
of those prostitutes. If that is right, the texts concern men involved with
homosexual prostitution, whether as prostitutes or clients, and not men
engaged in same-sex intercourse per se. But the term may also include a
reference to male youths in the pederastic relationships that were common
in Greek culture. As to "male-bedder," that term does not appear earlier
than these passages in any Greek literature that has survived, and the "bed-
der" part of it may well be vulgar slang—not unlike the "f-word" in English.
This is probably why the term *arsenokoitēs*, lacking literary elegance, does
not appear in earlier Greek literature that has survived, though it could well
have been the language of the street. So I'm inclined to take these texts to
refer pejoratively to specific Greek and Roman cultural homosexual practices, including prostitution and pederasty. I would need more definitive
proof that the Greek terms refer quite generally to persons involved in any
form of male homosexual sex per se to be able to say that these passages
forbid male same-sex monogamous relationships. So I'm setting these texts

aside as inapplicable to the kind of relationship James and I will have once we're married.

DAVID: I agree that our standard English Bible translations tend to be much too definitive in the use of such paraphrases. If I recall, around 2008 or so the publishers of an earlier version of a popular contemporary English translation as well as those of an update of a venerable classic English version were sued because they translated *malakoi* and *arsenokoitai* as "homosexual offenders" and "homosexuals" and "sodomites" respectively. The suits, brought by a gay man, charged that these translations—and thus, as far as he was concerned, the Bible—caused great emotional distress to gay men like himself. The suits were eventually thrown out, but it shows that translators can't be too careful with how they translate sensitive Greek terms.

PHILIP: Yes, I remember reading about that.

DAVID: Even so, I am not at all sure that these terms, even if they are pejorative, refer only to male homosexual practices all of us would disapprove of. I think the referents of these terms are more inclusive and more general, but I'll wait my turn next week to explain why.

STEPHANIE: Thanks for opening up this translation issue for us, Phil. Do you want to go on with your account of other biblical passages?

PHILIP: I do. So last but not least, I want to take a careful and extended look at the Romans 1 passage. I want to focus on parts of this passage where I take exception to Amanda's interpretation and explain why I do. I'm going to call the reading of Romans 1:18–32 that I offer a "contextualized" reading of the passage, contrasted with the reading Amanda gave last week, which I would call a "decontextualized" reading.

AMANDA: Can you explain that?

PHILIP: Yes. It seemed to me that you were lifting the passage out of its context in Paul's letter to the young Roman church and treating it as a self-standing discourse about what the Bible (and therefore God) thinks of homosexuality. You called it the consequence of God's giving up on humanity in response to humanity's rebellion against him, known as the fall. So, you said, left to their own devices, their religious apostasy expressed itself in moral perversity and depravity, the clearest and most graphic manifestation of which is homosexuality. You noted the uncompromising and sweeping language Paul uses to denounce it. You made it sound as though this is the Bible's manifesto against homosexuality, which Christians need to make their own if they are to have a "biblical" view of homosexuality.

AMANDA: Well?

PHILIP: My objection to that, Amanda, is that you are taking this passage out of its various contexts: its theological context in Paul's overall argument in Romans 1–3, its rhetorical context in how Paul structures that argument, and its historical and cultural context in first-century Rome and the broader Greco-Roman world. I think that is a serious misuse of Scripture. My contextualized reading looks at the passage very differently and arrives at a very different application of the passage to our question.

DAVID: Okay, can you give us that reading?

PHILIP: Yes. Let me begin my account of Romans 1 with Paul's declaration of the gospel in verses 16 and 17, with particular emphasis on those for whom that gospel is Good News:

> For I am not ashamed of the gospel, for it is the power of God for salvation to *everyone who believes, to the Jew first and also to the Greek.* For in it the righteousness of God is revealed from faith for faith, as it is written, "The righteous shall live by faith."

Throughout the epistle to the Romans—indeed throughout his epistles in general, Paul, like most first-century Jews, thinks of humanity as comprising two groups: Jews, who are God's chosen people with whom God has a special covenant, and gentiles (often, as here, referred to as "Greeks") who stand outside of this privileged relationship. His core message is that in Christ, God has created a new unity that transcends this duality to the point of rendering that duality irrelevant (Galatians 3:28). So, with this noted, let me continue with the next eight verses (vv. 18–25) that precede any mention of homosexuality and set the context for Paul's statements about it.

For the wrath of God is revealed from heaven against all ungodliness and unrighteousness of men, who by their unrighteousness suppress the truth. *For what can be known about God is plain to them, because God has shown it to them. For his invisible attributes, namely, his eternal power and divine nature, have been clearly perceived, ever since the creation of the world, in the things that have been made. So they are without excuse. For although they knew God, they did not honor him as God or give thanks to him, but they became futile in their thinking, and their foolish hearts were darkened. Claiming to be wise, they became fools, and exchanged the glory of the immortal God for images resembling mortal man and birds and animals and creeping things . . . [T]hey exchanged the truth about God for a lie and worshiped and served the creature rather than the Creator, who is blessed forever! Amen.*

My first question is: *what population is Paul describing in these verses?* First, they are said to possess a type of knowledge of God based on what God has revealed to them through his works of creation, or what we would call nature. Theologians call this God's *general* revelation, as opposed to God's *special* revelation—God's direct speech or communication through visions or prophecy to a particular audience. Even as recipients of God's general revelation, though without his special revelation, these people are "without excuse": they cannot claim that their knowledge of God through nature is insufficient, and they are held fully accountable for how they respond to the revelation they have been given. Second, they refuse to acknowledge what they know, and refuse to honor God as God and to give God the thanks that is his due. They deliberately suppress "the truth," the knowledge they have, with the result that they became fools, their hearts darkened. Third, they redirect their worship away from the true God, their creator, and toward false ones, worshiping created things and making them idols: human beings and various animals. So who are these people who do this?

AMANDA: All of us, surely, ever since the fall of Adam and Eve. They were the first to rebel, and we've inherited their rebellious hearts. That's what's called "original sin," and it has contaminated every last one of us. As I said last week, homosexuality is the result of humanity's universal rebellion against God.

PHILIP: But put yourself in the context of the young church at Rome to whom Paul is writing, Amanda. New believers in Christ, some with Jewish backgrounds and some with gentile backgrounds, make up this new group. In the eyes of the Jewish Christians it is Jews who worship the true God and who are God's chosen people. Gentiles, on the other hand, worship false gods, idols—sun gods, river gods, gods in the forms of human beings and animals. It is to Jews, not gentiles (Greeks), that "the oracles of God," God's *special* revelation has been entrusted (Romans 3:2). It is to Jews that "the adoption, the glory, the covenants, the giving of the law, the worship, and the promises" belong (Romans 9:4). The Jews rightly thought of themselves as having been privileged by God's special revelation, God's direct and personal communication with them. The gentiles, on the other hand, have received no such communication from God. What did *they* have by way of communication from God? And what did they do with it? These eight verses say it all.

DAVID: Ah, I think I see where you're going with this. You want to say that the verses describe not humanity in general, but the gentiles in particular.

PHILIP: Exactly, Dave. Paul's Jewish converts would never have recognized themselves in the description of the people in these eight verses. They knew exactly whom Paul was talking about. And so should we.

DAVID: I have a couple of problems with this way of reading the text, Phil. First, it seems like you're saying that apostasy and idolatry are exclusively gentile phenomena. But didn't the Jews have their own issues with apostasy and idolatry as well? The history of the Jews' relationship to God is replete with instances of idolatry, beginning with the golden calf in the desert and persisting throughout the rest of Old Testament history during the periods of their judges and kings—the worship of Baal, the Ashera poles, the "high places." So it seems much more likely to me that the indictment in the passage you just cited applies equally to Jews and gentiles, and that Amanda is right in taking the passage to apply to humanity universally, not just to gentiles specifically. Second, if Paul *were* focusing exclusively on gentile apostasy and idolatry in the passage, why doesn't he just say so?

PHILIP: Fair enough, Dave. Here are my thoughts on your first point. There's no denying that apostasy and idolatry were serious issues for God's Old Testament people as well. In fact, Paul will go on to say that Jews are guilty of the very same offenses they hold against the gentiles (Romans 2:1–4). But, as the Old Testament makes abundantly clear, Jewish apostasy and idolatry is a rebellious response to a *supernatural* knowledge of God's will, given uniquely to God's covenant people as *special* revelation. We read that God explicitly commanded them "not to have any other gods before [him]" (Exodus 20:3–4). That's very different from the suppression of a *natural* knowledge of God available from God's *general* revelation in creation. And while it is true that in both cases the groups in question (gentiles and Jews) are rejecting a knowledge that they had been given, leading them to substitute false gods for the true God as the objects of their worship, it is equally true that there are distinct versions of this. So when Paul describes the apostasy and idolatry of the population he's talking about in this passage, which of these two versions is the one in question? And of which of the two populations is it an accurate description?

DAVID: Well, if you're going to distinguish two versions of apostasy and idolatry based upon a distinction in the type of knowledge of God that is being rejected, I guess it's pretty clear that it's the version that suppresses a natural knowledge of God based on his general revelation, not the one that consists in disobedience to specially revealed commands in the context of God's covenant with his people. So yes, I agree that Paul has gentiles primarily in mind in Romans 1.

PHILIP: Moreover, Paul goes on to say that the consequence *par excellence* of the apostasy and idolatry he's referring to is God's abandoning the population that commits it to homosexual passions and actions. There are also other forms of depravity that he mentions later (see Romans 1:29–31), but this is the one Paul starts with and highlights. It is the emblematic consequence of the apostasy and idolatry he's talking about. Yet where in the Old Testament record do we see any lapse into homosexual depravity that results from *Jewish* apostasy and idolatry?

DAVID: You're right. It *is* striking that there is no record in the Old Testament of outbreaks or even instances of homosexual sin among the Israelites after the law—including the Leviticus passages we've looked at— was given to them in the desert. Of course that doesn't mean that such behavior didn't occur at all, but it does mean that it was never in the record and so not part of the collective memory of first-century Jewish people.

PHILIP: The Old Testament is quite clear about the consequences of Jewish apostasy and idolatry, leading to God's abandonment of them: it is captivity, deportation, exile, and subsequent domination by foreign powers, not homosexual depravity. Moreover, in the religious landscape of first-century Judaism we hear next to nothing about Jewish idolatry in the Old Testament sense. Neither Jesus nor Paul issues any warnings against converting from Judaism to belief in the Greco-Roman gods, much less the Canaanite gods, and participating in their cultic rituals. The religious movements within the Judaism of that period featured groups like the Essenes and the Pharisees who sought to purify the worship of the true God and ratchet up their obedience to him. Post-exilic Judaism seems to have been chastened of the devotion to foreign idols so characteristic of their pre-exilic ancestors. So for first-century Jews, religious apostasy and idolatry were ancient history.

DAVID: Okay, but what about my second point? If Paul is describing gentiles in particular and not humanity in general in the verses you cited, why doesn't he just say so?

PHILIP: Probably because he doesn't want to let Jews off the hook even at this point in his argument. As you've rightly pointed out, the gentiles had no monopoly on apostasy or idolatry. Paul wants to say that *all people*, regardless of their ethnicity and type of knowledge of God, are guilty of rebelling against the true God and substituting false worship for true, even if it is also true that this looks different for gentiles than it does for Jews.

AMANDA: So you're saying that the homosexuality condemned in the verses that follow the passage you cited is the consequence not of a universal human rebellion, but more narrowly of a *gentile* rebellion?

PHILIP: That's exactly what I'm saying, Amanda. Paul is depicting homosexuality as a manifestation of *gentile* depravity, not of the universal "original sin" that besets all of humanity, as you claimed last week. The oft-repeated claim that "homosexuality is a result of the fall" is not supported by this passage, the way I see it.

STEPHANIE: It may still be true in some sense that homosexuality really is "a result of the fall," but I agree with Phil that the Romans 1 passage doesn't teach this. I will have something to say about that when my turn comes.

PHILIP: Wow, Steph. Glad to hear that you're part of the conversation and not just monitoring it.

STEPHANIE: I love reflecting on what I'm hearing as our conversation moves along. I'm so thankful to God that the tone of our interaction remains friendly. I'm just very hopeful.

PHILIP: Amen to that, Steph. Let me go on. Now why does Paul paint such a devastating picture of the gentiles? Is it his purpose to write a theological tract on homosexuality, to guide the church in determining what "position" to take on the "issue"? Far from it. So here's the theological context. Paul is making a theological case for the conclusion that *all* have sinned and fallen short of the glory of God (Romans 3:23). Who are these "all"? They are *both* Jews *and* gentiles—or, to put it slightly differently, not only gentiles but Jews as well. The entire argument that begins with Romans 1:18—prefaced, as we saw, by Paul's declaration in v. 16 that the gospel is good news for *both* Jews *and* gentiles—right to the end of that chapter is the first stage of that case: gentiles have sinned in suppressing their knowledge of God, and as a consequence God abandoned them to a descent into utter moral depravity. But what about Jews? *They* don't do any of these things, do they? Aren't they God's chosen people, living morally upright lives? They have God's law, don't they? They are the children of Abraham, aren't they? How could *they* possibly have "fallen short of the glory of God"?

DAVID: I get it. So in chapter 2 Paul turns the table on the Jews. Is that what you mean by the "rhetorical context"? The Jews have been listening to Paul's condemnation of the gentiles, nodding their morally superior heads with approval. But then Paul abruptly takes aim against their hypocrisy. "In passing judgment on another you condemn yourself, because you, the judge, practice the very same things. Do you suppose—you who judge those who practice such things and yet do them yourself—that you will escape the judgment of God?" (Romans 2:1, 3).

PHILIP: Exactly right, Dave. Notice how Paul refers to the population described in chapter 1 as "they" and "them," but to the Jews in chapter 2 as "you," suggesting that these populations are distinct. It's as though his accusing finger pivots 180 degrees from "them" to "you." In fact, if we were editing Paul's letter we could title the first stage of the case, "The Depravity of the Gentiles," and the second stage, "The Hypocrisy of the Jews." Jews not only commit these same sins of depravity as the gentiles but, on top of that, they have made themselves oblivious to that fact—that's their hypocrisy! So both gentiles and Jews stand in desperate need of the grace of God. The news that this grace is available to both groups through the atoning death of Christ on the cross is the good news that is "the power of God for salvation to everyone who believes, to the Jew first and also to the Greek [gentile]" (Romans 1:16).

AMANDA: I'm not sure, Phil. I'm not ready to agree with your point that Paul is not here talking about the (universal) fall and its consequences, as I've always thought. I have to admit that your point is challenging, though. But, even granting the point, how does it relate to the issue of homosexuality—to the way you and I are called to live our lives as same-sex attracted individuals?

PHILIP: It doesn't, Amanda! It doesn't relate to us at all! Paul is not giving an abstract theological discourse on the effects of gentile rebellion against God, leaving his audience to simply imagine what those effects might look like. So here's the historical-cultural context. Remember that this is the young church at Rome he's writing to. This body of new believers in Christ, both Jew and gentile, was literally surrounded by monuments to pagan idolatry. Temples to pagan deities of all sorts could be seen everywhere throughout the Roman world. The cult of the emperor was the pinnacle of Roman idolatry. Situated in the middle of Rome was the Pantheon, an "all god" temple that still stands today as a tourist attraction. Crafted images of those deities (including statues of emperors), objects of worship and veneration, were on display all over the city. There's the idolatry. As for the homosexuality, what was going on in Rome and throughout the empire? An assortment of unbridled sexual activities, homosexual as well as heterosexual, was at the heart of Roman social life. The Roman aristocracy indulged in sex parties at their villas that involved both hetero- and homosexual debauchery. Even at the imperial palaces these orgies were the order of the day. The late great Emperor Gaius Caligula was notorious for his personal sexual excesses—with members of both sexes—and for the parties he hosted, which were nothing but sexual orgies. If you were a male guest of the emperor at one of these parties, take your pick: boys over here, girls over there. Caligula came to his own bad end by being stabbed to death, with the *coup de grâce* reportedly delivered to his genitals—no doubt by someone who was more than mildly offended by his sexually abusive behavior! In addition, the common Greek practice of pederasty, where an older free male "loved" a yet beardless youth and assumed the role of a mentor to the youth, was an approved social practice widespread throughout the Greek and Roman world. All of this would have been familiar to the young community of Christians in Rome—or in Corinth or in Ephesus or any other major city in the Roman Empire.

STEPHANIE: I took a course in "Sex and Sexuality in Ancient Greece and Rome" last semester. Fascinating. The course was very popular. Among the topics we studied were the various homosexual practices in those cultures as well as the ways these practices were regarded by their societies. What you're saying agrees with what I've learned in that course.

PHILIP: It's this entire corrupt social world that Paul is roundly condemning in Romans 1, as Paul's ancient audience would have immediately picked up. The same-sex attractions that Amanda and I experience, and my forthcoming marriage to James, are of a totally different order altogether. And here's the kicker: the males who participated in these activities—the "active" ones at least—were for the most part married to women and had families. These men were not naturally same-sex attracted, but they made themselves so, by habitually indulging in these orgies, often assisted by a huge consumption of alcohol. As we might say, they developed a "taste" for homosexual sex the way a teenager might develop a taste for tobacco or alcohol—no kid ever enjoyed their first cigarette or first beer! Eventually they might even become addicted and lose all interest in heterosexual sex. These pagan men truly "exchanged" their natural heterosexual inclinations for homosexual ones. Does this describe you or me, Amanda? Tell me the truth.

AMANDA: No, I guess not. I've never been aware of any heterosexual attractions to begin with.

PHILIP: Paul is quite clear that the people he's talking about "exchanged" their natural heterosexuality for homosexuality. He uses this word three times: twice to describe the apostasy and idolatry of the gentiles, and once to describe the acquisition of homosexual desire and behavior patterns. We need to pay attention to that word. You don't *exchange* A for B if you don't have A to begin with. The gentiles couldn't have exchanged the truth about God for a lie if they didn't have that truth to begin with. Neither you nor I, Amanda, had any heterosexual attractions to begin with, so how could we be counted among people who acquired their same-sex attractions through an exchange?

AMANDA: Yes, I see what you're saying.

DAVID: Wait a minute, Amanda! Don't give in so easily. It may well be true that neither Phil nor you *individually* had heterosexual attractions to begin with, which you then gave up to acquire same-sex attractions. But, as I was saying last week, Paul is not speaking individually, but collectively. By rebelling against God, the group he's talking about—whether humanity in general or the gentiles in particular—as a whole has exchanged good things for bad things. In this case, the good thing in question is the natural heterosexuality with which they were originally created, and the bad thing the unnatural homosexuality that they took on. The members of the group participate in this exchange, even if it is not replicated in their own individual experiences. As for "exchange," this doesn't have to refer to a conscious, deliberate choice. For example, suppose Stephanie, say, goes to the beach but neglects to take her sunscreen and ends up getting severe sunburn. We could say that she "exchanged" her healthy skin for damaged skin, without implying that she *chose* to do so. It just happened to her as a consequence of her neglect. An exchange isn't necessarily a voluntary choice. It could be passive rather than active.

PHILIP: Ever the philosopher, Dave. But if the "exchange" that represents the group's descent into homosexuality isn't an active choice on their part, what about their prior exchanges, their exchange of the truth about God for a lie, or their exchange of the glory of God for images of creatures? Are these exchanges also something that "just happened" to them, passive rather than active? Don't we want to see the word "exchange" used consistently in all three of its occurrences, either all passive or all active?

David: Yes, I guess you're right about that. Paul depicts the pagan suppression of their natural knowledge of God and their turn toward idolatry as an active, willful choice for which they bear responsibility.

Philip: And also, if homosexual passions and behavior is a "collective" consequence of the suppression of their knowledge of God, how is it that by far the vast majority of the members of the group who are guilty as a whole of that suppression, does not in fact exhibit same-sex desires or engage in same-sex behavior? All are guilty, but only a very few get hit with the consequence? Does that make sense to you? How is it that some members in the group, a relatively small minority, get to actually experience the "exchange," which gives them a built-in engine to sin, while the majority escapes it? Why would this consequence of the collective rebellion descend on some and not all? Don't we believe that the consequence of Adam and Eve's sin in the garden—what we call original sin—afflicts all of us, not just some of us?

David: Others get hit with other consequences. Not everyone gets the same.

Philip: You know, Dave, this totally goes against the most natural and, to me, obvious reading of the text that I can hardly believe you're even entertaining it, much less defending it. To me it looks as though you are pressing that interpretation into the text in order to maintain a "position" on the issue our conversations are about.

David: Well, perhaps I can defend my take on the text better when my turn comes next week.

Philip: I sure hope so, Dave. Let me go on. So, when Paul speaks of homosexuality the way he does—using inflammatory language like "the lusts of their hearts to impurity," "the dishonoring of their bodies among themselves," "dishonorable passions," "consumed with passion," "men committing shameless acts with men," and so forth—we can imagine that scenes with sexual acts like the ones I've described were in his mind and would be evoked in the minds of the newly converted Roman Christians who were near-contemporaries of Caligula and his successors. Such scenes would have been particularly revolting for the newly converted Jews among them, since they had been taught from childhood that homosexual behavior was offensive to God and punishable by death (remember the Leviticus texts?). Clearly, Paul has such scenes in mind and he evokes them in his audience as well. And we, his twenty-first century readers, should be equally disgusted!

So here's my bottom line, Dave. We can't just transfer what Paul says about the morally revolting homosexual practices of the ancient Greek and Roman world and use it as a theological template by which to evaluate same-sex relationships today. What Paul says in Romans 1 fits his contemporary situation to a tee. We would all join him in his condemnation of those practices. And if similar homosexual practices were evident today— as I'm sure there are—we should all take a similar view of them. But our contemporary understanding of homosexuality in general is different from Paul's—for example, Paul shows no awareness of an inborn, persistent homosexual orientation, and he appears to have just assumed that all people come into the world with an original heterosexual orientation. I suspect that you and Stephanie will discuss these ideas later on, but let me say for now that the difference between what Paul knew in his time and what we know today about homosexuality is a game changer. It requires a complete reassessment of the morality of same-sex relationships, including same-sex marriage. To fail to appreciate this difference results in unwarranted judgment against gays and lesbians who are pursuing a same-sex marriage, like James and me. It profoundly distresses me to see that the vast majority of my fellow conservative Christian believers don't see any significant moral difference between James's and my relationship, and the homosexual orgies of ancient Rome. They throw us into the same moral cesspool!

AMANDA: I'm sorry, Phil. I do understand your anguish about this. But I hope you'll also understand why folks who think about homosexuality the way I do since my conversion have a point. That point comes in verses 26 and 27 of chapter 1, and you haven't addressed it so far. Here's the text:

> For their *women exchanged natural relations for those that are contrary to nature;* and the *men likewise gave up natural relations with women and were consumed with passion for one another.*

Let me say again that offhand I won't dispute your point that Paul is talking about the gentiles of his contemporary pagan Greek and Roman culture specifically and not about humanity in general. I will certainly need to think about that some more. But I also pointed out in my talk last week that verses 26 and 27 are at the heart of Paul's condemnation of homosexuality, and I do believe that what he says there applies to homosexuality universally—including the same-sex relationships you want to defend. Paul is saying that homosexuality *as such* is "contrary to nature." Along with the church throughout its history, I take that to mean that homosexuality per se, not just certain pagan practices involving homosexuality, is contrary to God's design for human sexuality. And also, homosexual sex is, in the nature of the case, not procreative. God creates human beings as male and female, each with sexual attraction to the other. Sexual attraction, not to mention sexual behavior, between men and between women is "contrary to nature," that is, contrary to God's design. I don't think we can read these verses any other way.

PHILIP: I'm glad you brought this up, Amanda. I do believe, however, that you're misreading these verses, and again, with respect, I also believe your appeal to "God's design" is misplaced. I've already stated and explained my doubts about your reading of Genesis 1 as teaching that God has a binary design for human gender and sexuality. I called it a "Platonic fiction," remember? But we've also promised ourselves that we would revisit this in future discussions. Aside from that point, I disagree with you that Paul is switching from the particular to the general, from condemning the various perverted homosexual practices specific to Greco-Roman culture to condemning homosexuality in and of itself. I think you misunderstand what Paul means by "nature." Paul here is not referring to a general human nature (as, perhaps, designed by God) but to the actual natures of the people who engage in the deplorable acts he describes. These pagan participants in homosexual acts are acting contrary to *their* natures. In other words, he is describing people whose natures are *hetero*-sexual as willfully abandoning their heterosexuality by indulging in *homo*-sexual acts, thereby fueling what *for them* would be "unnatural" passions. He's not even considering those who, like you and me, have *homo*-sexual natures. Again, Paul uses the term "exchange." As we've seen, having excluded the "passive" interpretation of this term, we are left with seeing the exchange here as a voluntary, intentional act. So the Roman aristocrats, let's say, although they are heterosexual males who have wives and children (and probably also mistresses), nevertheless at these parties, and possibly elsewhere, pervert their inborn, God-given heterosexual natures by firing up their sexual engines to indulge in homosexual debauchery.

DAVID: Wow, Phil. That's pretty heavy! I'm not sure I agree with your account of the distinction between "natural" and "unnatural" here—at least not without raising what for me are some serious questions about it, which I'll do next week. But thanks for such a clear statement of your view!

AMANDA: So is this what you meant last week when you said that a mixed orientation marriage is unnatural for the same-sex attracted person? That it would be unnatural for me to get married to Mike, because it would go against my "nature" as a same-sex attracted person? And that it would be *doubly* unnatural for you and me to get married, despite the fact that even such a marriage would still be "within the biblical rules"?

PHILIP: Yes, and this is the very scripture I had in mind when I said that I could prove my point from the Bible—a claim that so astonished Dave.

DAVID: I'm still astonished, Phil. I think you seriously misread Paul's use in this passage of the distinction between what is "natural" and what is "contrary to nature." But I'll get to that next week.

STEPHANIE: So, Phil, can you sum up your view about the biblical passages that speak to the issue of homosexuality? And perhaps after that can you say something about how you would defend your choice to marry James based on what you would take to be a biblical understanding of marriage?

PHILIP: Certainly. First, I do not believe God has a design for human gender and sexuality such that intersex people, gays and lesbians, and transgender folks are left out of that design. Genesis 1 does not require such a narrow interpretation. Second, like Amanda, I do not believe that the Genesis 19 and Judges 19 episodes of homosexual gang rape have anything to do with our question. Third, I believe that neither the Leviticus texts, the vice lists in 1 Corinthians 6 and 1 Timothy 1, or even Paul's vitriolic condemnation of homosexual passion and behavior in Romans 1 rule out the kind of relationship James and I are pursuing: a relationship between persons of the same sex consisting of a lifelong, exclusive commitment to each other, based on a public covenantal declaration of faithfulness similar to the declaration of marriage vows in a heterosexual marriage.

DAVID: But even if you're right about these texts (which I'm not necessarily granting!) it doesn't follow that the Bible permits same-sex marriage, does it?

PHILIP: You're right, so I'll go there next. Genesis 2 records the creation of Eve (the "woman") and her entering into a "one flesh" union with Adam (the "man"). That legitimately raises the question of whether a "one flesh" union is ever appropriate between two men or two women. And it's undeniable that in Matthew 19 Jesus does frame his teaching on marriage and divorce in terms of the Genesis account of the creation of male and female. And finally, yes, Ephesians 5 does model the relationship of the spouses in marriage on the relationship between Christ and the church, the husband reflecting the role of Christ to the church and the wife reflecting the role of the church to Christ. So how would I respond?

AMANDA: How would you indeed?

PHILIP: There is no doubt that no alternative to heterosexual marriage is to be found anywhere in the Bible. There are many forms of marriage that are, if not commended, at least tolerated in the Bible. These include polygamy, levirate marriage, marriage to a slave, a rape victim, or a prisoner of war. But it is never questioned that marriage is between one male and one (or more) female(s). The issue for us is not whether there are biblical texts that afford a positive glimmer of a possible same-sex marriage, but whether or not same-sex marriage is ruled out by biblical teaching on marriage. There are no texts I know of that explicitly rule it out. The reason is obvious: same-sex marriage is a recent phenomenon, not on the horizon of the ancient societies of biblical times.

STEPHANIE: Aren't there reports of same-sex marriages in ancient Rome? As I recall, the Emperor Nero is reported to have married two men on different occasions, once as the "bride" and once as the "groom."

PHILIP: These "marriages" were charades, Steph. Same-sex marriage was not a legal institution sanctioned by the state as an alternative to heterosexual marriage, in the way same-sex marriage is currently permitted by law in many countries, including the United States.

STEPHANIE: I agree; I just wanted to make sure we didn't overlook that qualification to your claim. You were saying that there are no biblical texts that explicitly rule out same-sex marriage. Are there any that *implicitly* rule it out?

PHILIP: That's what many people claim. These are the texts that Amanda cited as the basis for her claim that the Bible rules out same-sex marriage. So I will respond to her on these texts. But there are also critiques of same-sex marriage based not so much on an examination of biblical texts, but on a theology of marriage that Christian theologians in the course of church history, beginning with the Church Fathers, have developed. Authors of such critiques will typically argue that same-sex marriages cannot fulfill one or more of the purposes of marriage. The obvious one that is not fulfillable is, of course, procreation. So I will have to respond to those critiques as well.

AMANDA: Okay, what about the *"ezer kenegdo"* and "one flesh" union concepts in Genesis 2?

PHILIP: What I find compelling is that in that passage God's explicit reason for creating Eve is that "it is not good that [Adam] should be *alone.*" Adam has a need of companionship, of partnership, of someone to share his life with. Significantly, God does not say, "It is not good that Adam cannot procreate by himself. I will make him someone he can have offspring with." Procreation is not anywhere in sight in this passage. Companionship, partnership, mutual support is. So God creates Eve, who satisfies the requirement of being an *ezer kenegdo*—a "helper fit for" Adam. My question here is this: is it explicitly or even implicitly ruled out that another male might meet that requirement as well? Neither the *ezer* nor the *kenegdo* mandates that the individual fulfilling that role must be someone with whom Adam can procreate. In James's and my case, for example, we will certainly be "helpers" to each other by coming alongside each other and, both of us being gay, we are *kenegdo* to each other in a way that an opposite sex spouse for either of us could not be. There is no "fitness" between a gay person and a straight person. So I don't see that the passage mandates that spouses be of the opposite sex. Second, does the "one-flesh" union require one party in that union to be male and the other female? I don't see that it does. The "one flesh union" is the complete union of bodies, hearts, and minds, each totally loving and surrendering to the other in a permanent bond of unity. We do tend to think of a male-female union as the paradigm case of such a union, but that's not enough to conclude that same-sex unions are excluded.

AMANDA: What about the passage in Matthew 19, where Jesus bases his teaching on marriage on the distinction between male and female?

PHILIP: It is certainly true that in that passage Jesus does that. He is reminding his hearers of the creation account in Genesis 1:27–28. The main point of the Matthew passage, however, is that marriage is intended by God to be permanent; divorce is not part of God's design. By framing his teaching on the creation of male and female "in the beginning" Jesus is taking for granted the accepted paradigm of male-female marriage that we find throughout the Bible. I doubt that he is saying that marriage *must* be a male-female relationship.

DAVID: Hmm. I'm not sure that Jesus isn't saying more than that, Phil. What's your take on the Ephesians 5 passage?

PHILIP: First, we should note that the Ephesians 5 passage puts the marriage relationship in the framework of "mutual submission" (Ephesians 5:21). A husband and his wife are to submit to each other: she by putting his interests above her own, and he by sacrificing himself for her. The relationship between Christ and the church is the model for that. They also submit mutually. The church submits to Christ by lifting him up as her Lord and living to serve him, and Christ submits to the church as his beloved bride by sacrificing himself for her. There may be different ways of submitting, but the overall message is clear: submit to and sacrifice for each other. James and I are not going to spend much time trying to figure out who is the Christ-figure in our marriage and who is the church-figure. That would be to miss the point of the Ephesians 5 passage. The message is for me to submit to James and for him to submit to me—that is, for both of us to put the interests and the good of the other above his own, and to sacrifice ourselves—including laying down our lives—for each other. And that's what we're committed to doing.

AMANDA: You said that there are also objections to same-sex marriage based on theologies of marriage developed by the Church Fathers and others. What are these objections, and how would you respond to them?

PHILIP: These theologies include procreation as an essential element of marriage. Obviously same-sex marriage is not procreative, so in the view of these theologians same-sex "marriage" can't really be marriage. I can't disagree that it is not procreative, though this deficiency can be remedied by adoption. James and I have discussed this, but we haven't come to an agreement on whether to adopt and if so how many kids we'd like to adopt. That's certainly something we'll figure out before we tie the knot. Same-sex couples cannot both be natural parents to their children, but they can certainly become (adoptive) parents! So, we ask, what is the big deal about lack of procreative potential? There are many heterosexual couples that know even before they marry that they are infertile for one reason or another. There is no prohibition against their marriage. Adoption is often suggested as a beautiful solution to their infertility. Procreation is never mandated in the Bible as part of the marriage obligation. Love and lifelong faithfulness are the hallmarks of biblical marriage. And there is no reason to think that same-sex couples cannot exhibit both of those as well as heterosexual couples.

STEPHANIE: Speaking of the purposes and benefits of marriage, isn't one of the other benefits of marriage that of containing sexual temptation? In 1 Corinthians 7:9 it says, "It is better to marry than to burn [with passion]."

PHILIP: Indeed. Both in the Bible and in church tradition marriage is also recommended as a solution to those who are subject to sexual temptation—which includes by far the great majority of us, whether we are straight or gay. Access to sexual intercourse within marriage helps straight people avoid the destructive pitfalls of lust and sexual license outside of marriage. But what recourse do gay people have? The consensus among conservative Christians is to deny gay people this benefit of marriage and to require sexual abstinence in all circumstances. But what if gay folks have no greater innate ability to resist sexual temptation than straight people have? In the Bible celibacy is a calling for those otherwise able to have sex. True, not every straight person able to have sex is provided with an opportunity to get married, even if they might want to be married. But they are not forbidden to marry. Others make a voluntary vow to be celibate that, from that time onwards, prohibits them from having sex. But what is there for gays and lesbians who are sexually able, have opportunity, are under no voluntarily undertaken vow, and feel neither called to nor gifted for a lifetime of sexual abstinence? A lifetime of cold showers?

So that's it. James and I will be married this summer. We believe that we have done our due diligence, both biblically and theologically. We have prayed about this, asking for God to guide us, even away from marriage if marriage is not God's will for us. We have listened to the counsel of other believers and to the "still small voice" speaking to our hearts. True, neither of us has heard an audible voice, as Amanda said she did. But we are both convinced that God has given us the green light, and we are very much looking forward to the new life God has for us. We want our marriage to be a witness for Christ and feel called to give hope to our many gay and lesbian friends who are on the edge of leaving the church altogether.

DAVID: Wow again, Phil. You seem to be as certain of God leading you to go forward with your marriage to James as Amanda is of God telling her directly that homosexual activity of any kind is sin and so forbidden. All I know is that God does not have it both ways. Either you are right and God blesses your plans, in which case Amanda has misheard God, or she is right and you are in serious jeopardy. You'll remember that I expressed some skepticism to Amanda about her account. So I need to be equally doubtful about your claim that God has given you the green light on your marriage.

PHILIP: No worries, Dave. I'm fine with that. I said at the time that the "caveat" you applied to Amanda's story would apply to mine as well. I believe we need to cut each other some slack. Amanda and I should both be free to follow in the direction that each of us is convinced God is leading us. Perhaps I should say it more strongly: we *ought* to follow in those directions, however they diverge and however mystified we might be at God apparently leading us in opposite ways. This is not relativism. It is an admission of our fallibility, our liability to misunderstand God's ways. While the Bible remains infallible, our interpretations of it will always be fallible. So we should adopt a posture of generosity and humility toward those who read the Bible differently from the way we do, instead of a spirit of judgment and finger wagging, even while we remain convinced of our own positions. "Each one should be fully convinced in his [or her] own mind" (Romans 14:5).

STEPHANIE: That's no easy task, Phil. But I do believe you are right. And it may help in finding a way out of the impasse of heated argument and counterargument that we find in so many conservative Christian communities. We should all take a deep breath, pause, pray, and move forward by being quick to listen and slow to speak. Thanks, Phil, for your presentation tonight. I think it's time to wrap up. Next week we'll have Dave's presentation.

AMANDA: Before we leave I just want to say that I respect your position, Phil, and the clear and forceful way you've presented it. But your way of reading many of the biblical passages seems very contrived to me, almost—and I hope you don't mind me saying this—as though you don't want to let the Bible speak for itself, but you're making it say what you want it to say. I'll think a lot about what you've said over the next week, but I should tell you that much of it doesn't ring true to me right now. Some of it does, but much of it doesn't. Maybe by next week I'll be able to put my finger on my concerns.

PHILIP: Well, I'm certainly up for that, Amanda. If there's anything I want more than being married to James it's being aligned with God's will for my life.

DAVID: I'm looking forward to next week as well. I share Amanda's concerns to a degree and I also have others of my own, and I'd like to put them out for discussion at that time.

STEPHANIE: All right then. Have a great week, everyone!

Questions for Reflection
and Discussion on Dialogue 2

1. Can you identify with any aspect of Philip's story? What strikes you as significant about his story? How does it challenge any stereotypes you may have about gay people, especially gay Christians?

2. What is Philip's account of God's "creation order" in Genesis 1, and how does his account challenge the "binary" character of Amanda's account? With whom do you tend to agree more? Why?

3. How does Philip's account of the Leviticus texts differ from Amanda's? With whom are you inclined to agree more? Why?

4. Philip makes an important point about the translation of the vice list passages in 1 Corinthians 6 and 1 Timothy 1. What is that point and how important do you think it is? Do you agree with his view that these terms, literally translated, condemn certain pagan homosexual practices and not homosexuality in and of itself? Explain.

5. Philip contrasts his reading of the Romans 1 passage with Amanda's reading. He claims that her reading is "decontextualized," while his reading is "contextualized." What is this distinction? Explain the "three contexts" that Philip draws attention to in his reading of the passage: theological, rhetorical and historical-cultural. How does each of these contexts apply to the overall interpretation of the passage?

6. David and Philip disagree about whether the descent into homosexuality and other vices described in Romans 1 concerns gentile apostasy specifically (Philip) or human apostasy generally (David). As you study the passage and what follows it in Romans 2 and 3, why is this difference of interpretation important and with whom are you more inclined to agree?

7. Philip tells Amanda that the Romans 1 passage on his interpretation "doesn't relate at all" to how he and Amanda are called to live their same-sex attracted lives. Why does he say this? Do you agree?

8. What is the difference between the active and the passive senses of "exchange" in the Romans 1 passage? Which of these two senses do you take to be operative in that passage? What are the implications of this difference?

9. Philip argues that same-sex attractions and even same-sex behavior are not "contrary to nature" for same-sex attracted individuals; these attractions and this behavior are contrary to nature only for heterosexually attracted individuals. Do you find his interpretation of the "contrary to nature" phrase in this context persuasive? Why or why not?

10. Explain how Philip's interpretation of the "fitting helper" and "one flesh" concepts in Genesis 2 and his interpretation of the marriage relationship taught in Ephesians 5 do not rule out same-sex marriage. Do you find his interpretation plausible or persuasive? Why or why not?

11. In your view, has Philip made an effective case for his view that the Bible does not prohibit his forthcoming marriage to James? What are the strengths and weaknesses of his case?

Dialogue 3

The four friends meet again the following Friday night.

STEPHANIE: Hey guys, I hope you've all had a good week. Thanks for coming out again tonight to continue the conversation we began two weeks ago. I think we've made good progress the last two weeks with Amanda's and Phil's presentations, both in tone and in substance. Let me pray for us. *Stephanie prays.*

> Father God, thank you for calling us into a relationship with you through the love and sacrifice of Jesus. Thank you for placing this subject on our hearts and please continue to guide us by your Holy Spirit. I pray for David tonight, that you would give him calm and clarity as he presents his thoughts, and that you would give all of us eagerness to engage with the ideas he presents and give him the feedback that is truly helpful to him and the rest of us as we continue to seek your direction on our conversations. In Jesus's name, Amen.

Dave, are you ready to tell your story and give an account of how you see the Bible speak to the issue of homosexuality and same-sex relationships?

DAVID: My story will be very short; in fact, it's really not much of a story at all. I grew up in a strong Christian family. My parents were missionaries and I was born overseas. Shortly after my younger brother Greg was born, my parents decided to come back to the States. They did not want us to be sent to missionary boarding schools, some of which were under investigation for child abuse at that time. So, when I was five years old, my dad took a job as pastor at one of the churches that had previously supported my parents on the mission field. My mother home-schooled me through eighth grade, and I attended the local public high school after that. My dad took another pastorate in another state during my senior year in high school, and so my parents and Greg moved; but I was allowed to stay with a church family in our town to finish high school.

Even though I had grown up in the church, having made a decision to follow Christ and be baptized within the first year of my dad's pastorate, my faith was pretty passive. As a home-schooled Christian kid, I faithfully attended the Sunday school classes at our church (my parents certainly saw to that!) and had only Christian friends who, like me, lived a pretty sheltered life in our little subculture. I was a good kid, believed the right things, didn't rebel, and did what was expected of me.

Prior to high school I did not know that there was any such thing as homosexuality. My father never preached on sexuality of any kind. Sex seemed to be a forbidden subject. The only conversations about sex that I was aware of were those among seventh- and eighth-grade boys, and those consisted mostly of observations of the physical attributes of the girls we knew. I remember once paging through a pornographic magazine that one of the other boys had gotten hold of and becoming sexually aroused at seeing those images of unclad women. It made me feel very uncomfortable and guilty afterward. The images were impossible to get out of my head.

As a high school freshman I was assigned to share a locker with a boy named Jay. He was nice and I liked him, but his mannerisms seemed somewhat affected. Not long after the beginning of school other boys were telling me, "Jay is gay." They also used some other language, which I won't repeat here. I had been so sheltered that I didn't even know what "gay" meant. My worldly-wise friends explained it in vulgar language laden with contempt. I understood what they were saying, but I could not imagine any boy being sexually turned on by another boy. Seriously? How does that happen? I decided that I would remain friends with Jay and not let this "news" about his sexuality bother me, and we remained friends through our high school years. His homosexuality never came up in our conversations, and I decided to ignore it in my relationship with Jay.

Not long afterwards, as my faith deepened and became more my own, I became more aware of the larger American culture and of conservative Christianity within that culture. I heard and read about "the need for American Christians to take a stand against homosexuality." Prominent Christian leaders were using their podiums of influence to proclaim that the Bible condemns homosexuality as sinful, that we should "love the sinner but hate the sin," and that we should support legislation opposed to "the homosexual agenda." I wondered if my friend Jay also heard such voices, and if so, how they affected him, but I never got up the nerve to ask him.

Coming to college I found out that the subject of homosexuality is controversial within the Christian community, that a few authors thought like Phil and were defending gay relationships on the basis of the Bible, while most other authors thought like Amanda and vehemently rejected those defenses as "unbiblical." Being a philosophy major I love thinking about issues that are controversial and trying to decide what side I'm most likely to be on. I cut my philosophical teeth on controversial philosophical issues (and nearly all of them are!). This led me to look at the issue of homosexuality and the Bible from all sides and come to some conclusions for myself on the subject. So that's where I am. My mind is open and I'm ready to be challenged, but as I told Phil last week, I'm no pushover.

STEPHANIE: Thanks Dave. Your story may be short, but it's important. I think more people will probably identify with your story than with those of the rest of us. Amanda and Phil, do you have any questions or comments on Dave's story before we proceed?

AMANDA: I'm good. I'm interested in hearing what Dave has to say about the biblical texts.

PHILIP: Same here. Go for it, Dave.

DAVID: Thanks guys. I'd like to respond, mostly to Phil but also to Amanda. I'll start with Phil, but I want to reverse the direction. I'll deal first with his defense of same-sex marriage and then respond to how he sees the biblical texts about homosexuality.

I don't think Phil's account of the biblical texts on marriage really works, and it seems to me that he's trying to wriggle out of taking them at their most likely (and, I would say, their obvious) meaning. The Ephesians 5 text does not work at all for a relationship between same-sex spouses. Despite Phil's somewhat dismissive attempt to minimize it, it *is* important within a marriage to distinguish the spouse who represents the role of Christ in Paul's analogy from the one who represents the role of the church. Otherwise the analogy falls totally flat. Paul speaks of the "one flesh" union between a husband and his wife as a "mystery," one that "refers to Christ and the church." Whatever we can say about the mystery of marital sex, and however much we want to emphasize *mutual* submission, the respective roles of Christ and of the church are distinct and asymmetrical. I don't think we need to get into the issue of "a wife's subordination to her husband" and that way of understanding the husband's "headship." I believe that there is plenty of room for debate on that issue. My point here only is that the relationship between same-sex spouses is necessarily symmetrical, whereas the relationship between Christ and the church is necessarily asymmetrical. For Paul's analogy to have any point, the spousal relationship has to mirror that asymmetry as well. So, I side with Amanda on this passage. I just find Phil's way of getting around the asymmetry very unconvincing. And if the "one flesh" relationship presupposes sexual difference here, as I'm convinced it does, I have to believe that it does in Jesus's reference to it in Matthew 19:5–6 as well, particularly since Jesus frames (I would say, grounds) his teaching on marriage on the creation "in the beginning" of male and female (v. 4). And if I'm right about this, then I think we should also conclude that the intent of the "mother text" in Genesis (2:24) on the one flesh relationship presupposes sexual difference as well.

PHILIP: Well, you're consistent. I'll give you that!

DAVID: I wish you could give me more than that, Phil. I wish you could say I'm right about that. Anyhow, as to the historic theologies Phil refers to, I don't identify as a Christian within the broader "catholic" communion that gives a measure of authority to tradition, as compared with the Protestant principle of *sola scriptura*, Scripture alone. I know that in those theologies—that of Augustine, for example—procreative capacity is often regarded as an essential element of Christian marriage. I do believe that procreation is a primary purpose of marriage, but I don't believe that procreative potential is an essential element of marriage. Years ago, just prior to their marriage, my uncle's fiancée contracted an illness that required the surgical removal of part of her reproductive system. They decided to marry anyway, and no one ever questioned the appropriateness or legitimacy of their marriage. My objection to same-sex marriage is based on biblical grounds, not church tradition.

PHILIP: Okay, for you same-sex marriage is out. So what's left for people who are same-sex attracted? Isolation? Perpetual loneliness? Is that healthy? Is that God's best for gay people?

DAVID: I think that the idea of "spiritual friendships" has merit. It's worth exploring.

AMANDA: Can you explain what that is?

DAVID: Sure. Some gay Christian authors who reject the idea of same-sex marriage as unbiblical have developed this idea in books and blogs. They point out that friendship is a rich and deep human experience, a gift from God recommended in the Bible and in Christian tradition and literature. They advocate non-sexual "spiritual" friendship relationships and bonds between all people, particularly between same-sex attracted people as an answer to the deep loneliness many gays and lesbians feel, partly as a result of their ongoing isolation within the Christian communities they long to be part of, and partly because they have chosen to forego marriage. So they form communal friendships.

PHILIP: I totally get that. Being part of a circle of friends whom you can trust with the deepest secrets and struggles of your life is a rich blessing. Does this idea also accommodate the idea of gay couples living together—in separate bedrooms, of course?

DAVID: So far as I can tell, the idea of "a chaste, gay couple" is controversial within the community of those who advocate spiritual friendship. One can easily see why. On the plus side, a couple who manages this successfully is open to receiving the blessings of a lifelong, stable committed relationship, as in a heterosexual marriage. On the minus side, the constant, unrelenting exposure to a situation from which sexual temptation is never absent, may be a struggle too hard for many celibate gay couples to endure.

STEPHANIE: Thanks for the "spiritual friendship" angle, Dave. An important option for Christian gays and lesbians committed to celibacy to explore. So now can you give us your take on the biblical texts on homosexuality?

DAVID: Okay. So let me begin with Romans 1. Phil gave us a powerful argument last week in support of his contention that in that chapter Paul attributes the descent into homosexuality not to human apostasy and idolatry in general but to gentile apostasy and idolatry in particular. I think he did a good job responding to the reservations I expressed at that time, so I don't want to relitigate that issue. And his contextual reading of the chapter—his attention to the theological, rhetorical, and historical-cultural contexts—makes sense to me. But I do think Phil is wrong in one component of his interpretation of that chapter, and that is the meaning of the "natural" versus "contrary to nature" distinction in verse 26. I'm with Amanda on that one.

PHILIP: Can you refresh us on Amanda's and my disagreement?

DAVID: Amanda took Paul to be saying that homosexuality in general is "contrary to nature"—that is, that homosexuality as such, and not just certain pagan manifestations of it, is contrary to human nature, to God's design for human sexuality. You, on the other hand, objected that by "nature" Paul does not mean general human nature (as, perhaps, designed by God) but the actual natures of the participants. You went on to clarify this by saying that Paul is describing people whose actual natures are *hetero*-sexual as abandoning their heterosexuality by indulging in *homo*-sexual acts, thereby fueling what *for them* would be "unnatural" passions that are contrary to the natures they individually have. You said that the passage does not even consider those who, like Amanda and yourself, have a *homo*-sexual nature.

PHILIP: So why do you think her way of taking it is right and my way of taking it is wrong?

STEPHANIE: It's tempting to just let Amanda take it one way and Phil another way and leave it at that. But that's not very satisfactory, nor very responsible. The important question is not in how many different ways we can "take" this text and then make an arbitrary choice among those ways, but to do our best to find out what Paul actually must have meant. To do that, we have to do some digging into the cultural and philosophical background of the distinction and see how other writers of the period use it. I've undertaken that kind of study myself, for a paper in the "Sex and Sexuality" course I mentioned, so if you don't mind, Dave, I'd like to take the lead on this topic next week. Are you good with that?

DAVID: Well, okay, I guess. So, with this loose thread left hanging, I'm done with my account of the Romans 1 passage. Before going on to look at the other biblical passages, though, I'd like at this point to raise some broader issues regarding homosexuality that haven't been explicitly addressed by any of us, though we've skirted around them. Two weeks ago, Amanda, you told us that you prefer the phrase "same-sex attracted" to the labels "gay" and "lesbian" because you disavow having a gay "identity." I'm sure you recall my protest and your response that as a Christian your identity is in the "new creation" that you have become in Christ. You admitted that your same-sex attractions are not gone—they continue to be part of your "flesh" that you are called to put to death every day—but you refuse to be identified by them.

AMANDA: Yes, of course I remember that. I also remember that you said you wanted to bring that up again.

DAVID: I do, and I want to put it into a larger context, that of the concept of *sexual orientation*. Phil alluded to this crucial concept last week, but we haven't so far given it a thorough look. This concept is a modern concept. There is no reason to think that it was current in biblical times or familiar to any of the biblical authors. The American Psychological Association defines "sexual orientation" as "an enduring pattern of romantic or sexual attraction (or a combination of these) to persons of the opposite sex or gender, the same-sex or gender, or to both sexes or more than one gender." When I was first introduced to it, the term "homosexual orientation" was used primarily, if not exclusively, to refer to persistent same-sex attraction. In the literature that I read, produced by writers within my conservative Christian culture, such an orientation was the result of a sin-laden situation: either the consequence of an individual's choice to participate in homosexual activities, resulting in an eventual addiction to those activities—like smoking or drinking or drugs—or the result of sexual abuse or patterns of family dysfunction. A homosexual orientation was something people acquired, an effect of "nurture," not "nature." People are not *born* gay, these writers insisted, but *become* gay. When later I read the autobiographies of a couple of gay Christian men and learned that their sexual attraction could not be attributed to any of those alleged causes, it came as something of a shock to me. Their first awareness of their own sexuality was of an attraction to other males, not to females. And this attraction persisted, despite their desperate attempts to pray it away, and despite going through multiple reparative therapy sessions. These authors pointed to prenatal biological causes such as hormonal imbalances affecting *in utero* brain development. Scientific research on this is ongoing, but it is by now well established that some gay people—probably the vast majority, if not all—are indeed "born gay." And if that is the case, if in most cases same-sex attraction and desires are hardwired into one's brain, such desires are involuntary, and you're not sinning when you experience them. And if you're not sinning, you have nothing to repent of— at least as far as your same-sex attraction is concerned. Your same-sex behavior is another story. Behavior involves choice and responsibility.

AMANDA: I'm not unaware of these developments in scientific research, Dave, though I have to confess to a good degree of skepticism about them. A single cause of same-sex attraction has not been proven, and the emphasis on "nature" over "nurture" strongly strikes me as overblown. In any case, as I've been saying, same-sex attractions are violations of God's design. It is inconceivable to me that God should create people with such violations of his design "baked in." As I've also been saying, the Bible is unequivocal and consistent in its condemnation of homosexuality as sin, and if I have to choose between what God says and what man says, I'll always go with God.

PHILIP: Wait a minute, Amanda. You said last week that you yourself never experienced heterosexual attractions to begin with, that the idea of "exchanging" heterosexual desires for homosexual ones is not an idea that describes you. You seem to be saying something different now.

AMANDA: Well, *something* must have happened during my preadolescence to awaken same-sex attractions in me. I don't know what it could be. My family life was good, even if we were not a Christian family. But there had to be *something*. God didn't create me with same-sex tendencies.

PHILIP: I'm sorry, Amanda. I can't buy that. The neurobiological scientific research is clear and even if it is still ongoing, the results to date are pretty conclusive.

DAVID: I don't buy it either, Amanda. Your way of thinking raises the huge question about what attitude Christians of biblical faith should have toward the inquiries and results of modern science. My own conviction is that we don't have to choose between the Bible and science or, as you put it, between "what God says and what man says." God reveals himself through both Scripture and nature, and where there is an apparent conflict we need to be discerning in interpreting both science and the Bible. Ever since Augustine the church has always insisted that "all truth is God's truth," wherever it is found, and in principle there cannot be real conflict.

AMANDA: Well, the history of the last several centuries has shown that when Christians try to harmonize science and Scripture, the Bible always loses; the Bible is interpreted through the "assured" results of science, not the other way around, and the voice of Scripture is diminished. No wonder our society has become increasingly secularized over time and the Bible all but cast aside.

STEPHANIE: This looks like another issue we'll need to revisit. For now, Dave, can you explain how your point about a homosexual orientation that in the vast majority of cases is inborn ties in with what you want to say about a "gay identity"?

DAVID: Yes. Here's the point: If your same-sex attraction is persistent and native to your very being, not the result of anything you did or anything that happened to you, then there is no shame in saying, "I am gay." And not only is there no shame, but you are probably aware that your gayness filters through to how you think, your emotional life, your social interactions and your perceptions of your natural environment, and even how you experience God. If you are a Christian, I agree with Amanda that your *ultimate* identity is that of a redeemed child of God. But there are levels of identity, some of which are more basic than others to your being the person you are. For example, Phil told us that he loves the outdoors—camping, hiking, mountain climbing. And he loves worship music. These are pretty important to who he is, but not as important as his being gay, which in turn is not as important to his being a child of God through Christ. Phil is a Christian, but not just a Christian who happens to be gay, or a lover of the outdoors or of church music. He is an outdoors-loving, church-music-loving, *gay* Christian. "Christian" is the noun, and the other aspects are adjectives. But some of the adjectives go deeper into the core of his being than others, and so are closer to the noun than others.

Philip: Dave, thank you. Thank you for the way you've put this. Most straight people, I've observed, are not nearly as conscious of their straight identity as gay people are of their gay identity, and so I hear straight people more or less rebuking me for "taking on" (!) a gay identity. But that rebuke misses the point just as much as the implied rebuke white people in America direct at black people when they say, "We should all be colorblind." Black people are much more conscious of their black identity than white people are of their white identity, because of the history of shaming and oppression they have endured. You could say much the same about gay people.

Amanda: So how does all this tie in with your reading of Romans 1? I thought you agreed with me and disagreed with Phil about what Paul means by "natural" and "contrary to nature"?

David: I do agree with you on that point, Amanda. Where I disagree with you is with your oft-repeated claim that the passage condemns same-sex *desire*, or *attraction*, as well as same-sex *behavior*. You've said several times that your persisting attraction to women and not only the same-sex activities of your pre-Christian past, is sinful. But the Romans 1 passage we looked at (and I thought we were done with for today) does not condemn same-sex attraction. What it condemns are homosexual "lusts" (v. 24) and "passions" (v. 26 and v. 27) as well as homosexual acts. Lusts and passions are not mere desires and attractions. It is one thing to feel a sexual attraction to someone; it is quite another to experience sexual lust and passion. As I've been saying, feeling a sexual attraction, whether gay or straight, is a manifestation of how we're wired. It is "non-culpable," not a sin issue. Crossing the line from attraction to lust and passion is a different matter, both in the case of non-marital straight sexual feelings and gay ones. I don't think you'll find a single text in the Bible where same-sex attraction as such is condemned as sinful.

Philip: So you're saying that it's okay to be gay, but not to act that way? That's like saying that it's okay to be a duck but not to quack.

73

DAVID: I don't want to be flip about it, Phil, but I do think that the passage does not condemn same-sex attraction as such, and that we should stop making such sweeping statements as "homosexuality is sin," which we hear often from people who take Amanda's point of view. She has said it often herself, in fact. It isn't biblically accurate and all it does is shame gay people. What we should say, in fact should insist on, is that homosexual *acts* are what's sinful as well as the heated *lusts* and *passions* leading up to those acts. Just as with straight people it's okay to be sexually attracted to someone but not to let that attraction spill over into lust and behavior when the person you're attracted to is not your spouse, so it is with gay people. There's a line between attraction and lust that should not be crossed.

STEPHANIE: I'm not at all sure you're right about it not being "biblically accurate," Dave. We need to look more closely at the language of the Romans 1 passages you cited. It's important to go beyond the conventional translations here and look at the original Greek, just as we had to do last week with the vice list passages in 1 Corinthians and 1 Timothy. Almost all contemporary English translations do translate the psychological nouns Paul uses in the passage as "lusts" or "passions," but that is to over-translate the original Greek terms. Paul uses three different terms to describe the emotional or affective states of the people he's describing. In v. 24 the Greek term is *epithumiai*. This is one of the most general terms in Greek for "desires." You will find this term correctly translated as "desires" in almost every other of its occurrences in the New Testament. In v. 26 the word used is *pathē*. This is the normal Greek word for "feelings" or "emotions" or, in the English of an earlier day, "affections." It may, but does not have to, refer to intense or irrational feelings. And finally, the Greek word in v. 27 is *orexis*. This is a near synonym of *epithumia*. It conveys a sense of "yearning" or "longing." In context I would translate it as "hankering." Again, it may, but does not have to, refer to an intense or irrational craving. Ancient Greek does not have a separate vocabulary for desires, affections, or hankerings on the one hand, and lusts and passions on the other. So these three words could describe same-sex attraction as well as same-sex lust and passion. The latter are not qualitatively different from the former. They are just more intense forms of the former, and Greek would show this by using modifiers (like "very" or "intensely"), which are not present in this passage. So, correctly translated, the psychological language in the passage in these verses is more accurately represented as follows:

Therefore God gave them up in the *desires* of their hearts to impurity . . . to dishonorable *emotions* . . . and the men . . . were
consumed with a *hankering* after one another . . .

There is certainly an emotional intensity to Paul's language throughout
the passage, because, as Phil showed us, Paul is in the process of graphically
describing the depravity of the gentiles to his mostly Jewish audience who
would naturally concur with that assessment of the moral state of the gentiles. But the present point is that Paul does not distinguish non-culpable
psychological states from culpable ones when it comes to homosexuality.
Not only same-sex lust and passion, but same-sex attraction and desire as
such are included in Paul's sweeping condemnation. So on this point I have
to agree with Amanda and disagree with you, Dave. Shaming or not, that's
what the passage actually says.

DAVID: But if Paul is describing the psychological states of the pagans who indulge themselves in the abominable practices Phil talked about
last week—pagans who perverted their God-given heterosexuality—and
not about the psychological states of persons who have a homosexual orientation in the sense I've just described, does his condemnation of those
particular pagan psychological states even apply to people today who are
homosexually oriented?

STEPHANIE: That's a great question, Dave. I'd say that in describing
homosexuality *as he knew and experienced it in his day* Paul does not dis-
sociate the sinfulness of homosexual desire or attraction from the sinfulness of homosexual behavior. But that doesn't necessarily mean that given
homosexuality *as we know and experience it today* we should follow him
there. Paul sees the homosexual desire and activity he observes in his pagan contemporary culture as the expression of a perverted and deliberate
choice—an "exchange," as we saw. We see homosexual desire and activity
for the most part as the expression of an unchosen and innate neurobiological condition. Whether or not you're right that "homosexual *acts* are
what's sinful"—that's something that still remains to be discussed—I have
to agree with you that same-sex attraction *as we know it today*, particularly
if it results from an inborn condition, is a non-culpable psychological state,
even as I accept Paul's condemnation of the homosexual "desires, emotions
and hankering" *of his pagan culture* as fully culpable.

PHILIP: It sounds like you're saying that the homosexuality Paul knew about in the first century is a different thing from the homosexuality we know about today.

STEPHANIE: I wouldn't call it a different "thing," Phil. I'd call it a different *construct*. In the same way, what we call "Hansen's Disease" today is a different construct from the leprosy described in the Bible in Leviticus 13. In biblical times leprosy was thought to be a punishment for sin, as indeed it was for Miriam (Numbers 12). There were social expectations and protocols applied to leprosy that do not apply to Hansen's Disease today. Hansen's Disease carries no social stigma as leprosy did in biblical times. People infected with Hansen's are treated with antibiotics and are not required to be isolated. They are certainly not required to present themselves to a priest or minister for examination to certify their healing!

AMANDA: Steph, I wouldn't be so quick to draw this distinction between what Paul knew and experienced of homosexuality in his day and what we know and experience of it in our day, and then summarily dismiss Paul's point of view as outdated. Do I have to remind you that Paul is the divinely inspired author of Scripture? Our contemporary views, even if they are based on scientific research, are not divinely inspired. That seems to me to be the height of arrogance: we know better than God! The Greeks have a word for that, Steph. That's *hubris*.

STEPHANIE: I'm sorry you think that, Amanda. This is not at all my motivation, and I don't agree that this is what I'm actually doing. I'll have to let it pass for now, but I'll have more to say about that next week. So let's move on. Dave, do you want to comment on the 1 Corinthians 6 and 1 Timothy 1 passages, and then the Leviticus texts as well?

DAVID: Yes, I do. And I'll also want to say something about Genesis 1. As for the "softies" and "male-bedders" (yes, I agree with Phil that those translations are more accurate than the usual paraphrases), I don't quite agree with him on the referents of those terms. He is inclined to take them to refer to the two parties involved in male homosexual prostitution and male pederasty. He may be right, but I'm more inclined to see the reference quite generally to those who are involved in any male homosexual activity. As Phil correctly pointed out, the term *arsenokoitēs* ("male-bedder") is not found in the extant Greek literature prior to Paul. My take on this is that it is likely that Paul invented the term. If, however, Paul were referring to the widespread practice of Greek pederasty, he would not have to resort to inventing a new term. He could have used the familiar terms *erastēs* ("lover") to refer to the older, active partner, and *erōmenos* ("beloved") to the "beardless youth," the passive partner. So there would be no need to invent new language. If, on the other hand, Paul did feel the need to invent new language (suggesting that he is *not* just referring to pederasty), that raises the question, what might have inspired Paul to invent the term *arsenokoitēs*? There is a probable answer, which is this: In the Septuagint, the Greek translation of the Old Testament that Paul would have been familiar with, the Greek translation of the literal Hebrew expression our English Bibles translated as "lying with (or having sex with) a male" is "going to bed with a male." So very likely Paul had the Leviticus scripture in mind when he invented the term *arsenokoitēs*. No one has suggested that the Leviticus language is restricted to the context of prostitution or pederasty, so to my mind it is more likely than not that Paul is referring to any male who has sex with another male. But I agree that this is not decisive by itself.

PHILIP: Just a minute, Dave. I need to interject here. I agree that Paul could have used the terms *erastēs* and *erōmenos* if he were *only* referring to Greek pederasty. But I think that he was primarily referring to homosexual prostitution, and only secondarily to pederasty, and possibly also to other perverse cultural practices like the orgiastic parties I mentioned last week. The pederasty terms would not have applied to situations involving prostitution and debauchery, which are devoid of any kind of "love." So he needed a broader umbrella term that would include both pederasty and prostitution as well as other perversions.

DAVID: Okay, Phil, point taken. As I said, I don't think the 1 Corinthians 6 and 1 Timothy 1 passages are decisive by themselves. When the meanings of Hebrew or Greek terms are contested, we should avoid basing doctrinal positions on them. As for the Leviticus texts, the description of male-male sexual intercourse as an "abomination," it won't do to suggest—as I think Phil came close to doing—that the reason this act is abominable is that it is practiced by such pagan nations as Egypt and Canaan. For this just pushes the question one step further back: presumably not everything these nations do is abominable, so there must be a reason for the "abomination" that goes beyond the mere fact that this act is practiced by these nations. And as to Phil's suggestion that the prohibition is against demeaning a man by degrading him socially—a prohibition that presupposes patriarchy—I don't see anything in the context to suggest that. The prohibition of male-male sex is quite general and unqualified. I think it is less "speculative" (Phil's term, you may recall) to suggest—as Amanda did—that the prohibition is grounded in the principle of the inviolability of the created distinctness of male and female. So I side with her on this point.

AMANDA: Thanks, Dave. I was beginning to feel very alone.

DAVID: Not only here, Amanda, but I also side with you in your reading of the creation account of "male and female" in Genesis 1. There is no difficulty in understanding how, in the creation of night and day as distinct from each other, the inclusion of the transitional phases of dawn and dusk is presupposed. Nor is the creation of amphibious animals, or estuaries and marshes precluded from the creation of land animals as distinct from sea animals, or the sea as distinct from land. But it is a stretch to extend this to include the creation of other (intermediate?) genders and sexual identities, as part of God's original design for humanity, as Phil has suggested. The idea that being gay or transgender occupy an intermediate spot between the poles of a spectrum, those poles being male and female, just doesn't make any sense. It might make some sense for intersex, but that's about it. With respect, Phil, this is in my opinion a very contrived way of making the Bible say what you want it to say. I do think it is important to try and figure out how being gay, transgender, or intersex fits into a theology of God's design for human beings as male and female, each with sexual desire for the other. The default explanation on offer is that these are somehow "results of the fall." I'm not totally happy with that and would love to think about that some more with you.

STEPHANIE: I hope we'll have a chance to do just that next week. Do you two have any questions or comments on Dave's presentation tonight? If not, I have one that I'd like to ask Dave about before we leave for the night.

DAVID: What is it?

STEPHANIE: In our first conversation, Amanda mentioned that she had enrolled in a "reparative therapy" program, and that while the program did not take away her same-sex attraction, it was helpful in reinforcing her decision to stay away from same-sex behavior and relationships. We noted at the time that this type of therapy was controversial and we decided that it should be put on our list of topics to discuss, but we haven't done so up until now. Now that we've talked more fully about the concept of "sexual orientation," I think we're ready to do so. I wonder, Dave, whether you have any thoughts about this subject.

DAVID: Sure. Let me say that, apart from the deceptiveness and manipulation that has now been exposed and that has discredited the practice of it, such therapy *in principle* is neither all good nor all bad. There are some testimonies—not many—of people who have been genuinely helped by it. My hunch is that people whose homosexual orientation is *not* due to an innate neurobiological condition but who later in life—whether through their own choices or through various things that happen to them—*become* homosexually oriented, might be helped by some kind of process that includes spiritual formation, counseling, and possibly appropriate therapies, if there are any. In such cases it might be possible to *restore* their sexual orientation to its original heterosexual state. I believe that many Christians who condemn same-sex attraction as in itself sinful believe—mistakenly, in my opinion—that a homosexual orientation *always* arises in this way, and therefore can in principle always be reversed. The hopes and expectations raised by this mistaken belief has, I'm convinced, done serious damage to many gay and lesbian individuals whose sexual orientation has been fixed from birth. But I admit that all this is just speculation on my part. I'm not aware of any scientific studies that have been done to confirm it, nor can I see how such a study might even be conducted so as to yield reliable results.

STEPHANIE: Amanda or Phil, do either of you have any comment on that?

PHILIP: I've had no personal experience with reparative therapy. Having been kicked out of my church I was never encouraged by my pastor to consider it, nor did anyone else recommend it to me. I've heard plenty of horror stories through my online chat partners. I'm horrified that such treatments as electric shock therapy were often part of its therapeutic regimen—as though homosexuality is a form of mental illness. I'm glad I was spared those experiences. It strikes me as just as misguided, even cruel, as the attempts of an earlier day to "repair" left-handedness.

AMANDA: My experience wasn't as horrifying as that of others, if their stories are true. And, as I explained, I did get some benefit from it, but it did nothing to eliminate my same-sex attractions. I want to endorse David's suggestion that spiritual formation and counseling may—at least in some cases—be successful in reorienting people toward a more biblical lifestyle.

STEPHANIE: Thanks, everyone, for your thoughts on this. There is probably more to be said on this subject, but we'll leave it here for now. Phil and Amanda, do you have any further questions for Dave on his presentation tonight?

PHILIP: I have a ton of questions and not a few rebuttals in mind, but I'll hold off until we've heard from Steph next week. For now I just want to say that I'm grateful to Dave for really understanding the issue of "gay identity."

AMANDA: I'm glad to see that Dave is more or less aligned with my way of taking the biblical passages. I do have a few questions, but will also hold off for now. I'm very curious about what Steph has to say, so I'll wait as well.

STEPHANIE: OK, we'll call it a night. It looks like I have my work cut out for me. See you all next week for our final conversation.

Questions for Reflection
and Discussion on Dialogue 3

1. With what aspects of David's story do you identify? If you are straight, what experiences have you had with gay people in your family or circle of friends? How have these experiences impacted your theological beliefs about homosexuality?

2. What is David's critique of Philip's account of the biblical passages (Genesis 2, Matthew 19, and Ephesians 5) that speak to marriage? How does he respond to Philip's claim that these passages do not rule out same-sex marriage? Do you agree with David's critique? Explain.

3. Explain David's concept of "spiritual friendships" as a possible solution for gay people who choose to remain celibate. What is the positive value of such friendships? What are its limitations, if any?

4. How does David challenge Philip's interpretation (though not his translation) of the "softies" and "male bedders" mentioned in the vice lists of 1 Corinthians 6 and 1 Timothy 1? Is his challenge effective? Discuss.

5. David agrees with Amanda against Philip on the interpretation of the Leviticus texts that prohibit male homosexual activity. In your view, is that prohibition grounded in God's creation order, as Amanda insists, or does it reflect a cultural norm not necessarily valid in our day? Explain.

6. How does David challenge Philip's account of God's creation order of human gender (and sexuality) in Genesis as non-binary? With whom do you tend to agree more?

7. David introduces the concept of "sexual orientation" into the discussion. He argues that in many if not most cases, a homosexual orientation is innate, a psychological expression of a congenital

81

biological condition, and thus non-culpable. If he is right, what difference does this make to one's moral evaluation of homosexual desire and behavior?

8. Stephanie challenges David's distinction between (one the one hand) same-sex attraction and (on the other) same-sex lust and passion, as biblically based. She argues that David's view of the former as "non-culpable" and of the latter as "culpable" cannot be supported by an accurate translation of the Greek words used in the Romans 1 passage. If she is right, what difference does this make to our interpretation of biblical teaching on homosexuality?

9. Crucial to Stephanie's account is a distinction between "what Paul knew and experienced of homosexuality in his day" and "what we know and experience of it in our day." She says that homosexuality as we know it today is a different "construct" from the homosexuality known in Paul's day. Do you agree? If not, why not? If so, is this difference important? Why?

Dialogue 4

The four friends meet again the following Friday night for their final conversation.

STEPHANIE: Good to see you guys one more time. I hope you've all had a good week.

AMANDA: Steph, thanks again for organizing these conversations. For me, some of what I've heard has been confirming, and quite a bit has been unsettling. But I'm glad we're doing this. We all need to be stretched in our thinking, whether we end up shifting away from our positions or not.

PHILIP: I agree. Too much conversation in the Christian community on this topic has consisted more of people *talking at* each other than people *listening to* each other. We're proving that the latter is at least a possibility, even if we don't end up agreeing with one another.

DAVID: Yes, for me too this has been a challenging series of conversations. We're certainly sharpening each other as "iron sharpens iron" (Proverbs 26:17). I've especially enjoyed the spirit of honesty and mutual respect that has characterized our times together. I'm sure that our decision to open with prayer has been the key.

STEPHANIE: I agree with you, Dave. Amanda, before we begin, would you pray for us?

AMANDA: Sure. *Amanda prays.*

Dear heavenly Father, thank you for your Word, which is a lamp unto our feet and a guide unto our path. Help us, Lord, in our thinking and our behavior not to be conformed to the world and its standards. Help us not to twist your Word in order to conform it to our own understanding. Our subject is difficult and challenging. Calm our hearts as we listen to one another, give us your Spirit to discern what is true and what is not, the courage to call out what does not conform to your Word, and the will to obey it. In Jesus's precious name, Amen.

STEPHANIE: Okay, let me begin with my story. Like Dave, I have never experienced same-sex attraction myself. But I have experienced the issue up close and personal: my twin sister Melanie is gay.

As kids Mel and I were like "two peas in a pod." Mel is dearer to me than my own life. "Mel-'n-Steph" is like a single name that we've always shared. We grew up in a loving home. Our dad is Jewish and our mom grew up Catholic. When it came to faith, our family fell between those stools. Our parents had a rather undefined faith in God, a sort of "common denominator" faith that respected both of their traditions while actively practicing neither. They had met in graduate school, and both earned their doctorates at the same time. They both found teaching jobs at the same liberal arts college in California, in different departments. As tenure track assistant professors they taught their classes and published their way (without perishing) toward tenure and promotion. Their circle of friends consisted almost entirely of faculty colleagues at the college. Their politics were liberal, though not stridently so. A few of their friends were conservatives so that made for some interesting conversations. After middle school Mel and I were sent to an elite private high school some distance away from home that was known for its rigorous classic curriculum in the liberal arts, and its high success rate in placing its graduates in the best colleges and universities in the country. I was introduced to both Latin and Greek there, and I took to those languages like a fish to water. Mel fell in love with art history. We parted ways when it came to choosing undergraduate schools, which I'll explain in a minute. I came here to major in classics, and Mel went to Cornell to major in art history. Both of us will graduate this spring and, as it turns out, we have both been accepted into our respective PhD programs at Berkeley—me in classics and Mel in art history (with a concentration in medieval art). So come this fall we'll be together again and closer to home.

Mel and I shared a suite together in the dorm at our private high school. The suites were arranged for occupancy for three students per suite, and so we found ourselves sharing the suite with a third student, Karen, who happened to be a Christian. The school had a Christian Fellowship group much like the one we're part of here, only suited to a high school context. Karen was a member of the Fellowship, and one day she asked us if we wouldn't mind her hosting a Bible study in our suite on Tuesday nights. We had no idea what that was all about, but after she explained it, we were both fine with it. We had plenty of things going on, and we were certainly willing to vacate the suite on Tuesday nights. We weren't in the least interested in joining the study ourselves, but it often happened that before we left to go to the library or wherever, the Bible study group members would arrive, and we'd chat for a while. I got to know them and like them. I noticed something about Karen and her Christian friends that I found very attractive. There was a quality to their lives that was different—one that I hadn't found in myself or in the lives of other students I was hanging out with. It wasn't long before I stopped going to the library and joined the study myself. The Bible study was on the Gospel of John. Reading, thinking, and talking about the words of Jesus and observing his interactions with people evoked in me a desire to know more about Jesus or, perhaps more accurately, a desire to *know* Jesus personally. Long story short: at a Fellowship group retreat I gave my life to Christ. This happened just before our seventeenth birthday.

AMANDA: Did Mel go with you to the retreat? Did she become a Christian as well?

STEPHANIE: I was about to get into that. It's time to share that part of my story. In my early teens, just before we were transitioning from our local middle school to the high school away from home, I began to notice boys in a new way. "Isn't Stevie the cutest?" I once said to Mel. I was ardently hoping that Stevie might notice me as well. By this time our parents allowed us to wear make up, and every morning I would put some on, hoping that my glossier lips, my shaded eyes and darkened eyebrows would be just the thing to catch Stevie's attention. I imagined going out on a date with him and dreamed about my first kiss with him. A serious crush! Mel, though, was totally unresponsive to my excitement about Stevie. "I'm happy for you," she replied apathetically. "I'm just not into guys the way you are." That's strange, I thought. We're twins, the same age, but maybe Mel isn't there just yet. But then, when she said, "I'm more into girls" and meant that in the way that I was "into" Stevie, I became totally alarmed. I knew something of what it meant for boys to be "into" boys and girls "into" girls, but I refused to believe that it was that way with Mel. *Mel gay? No way!*

By the end of our sophomore year at the high school Mel had developed her own life, apart from the life we had always shared together. She became secretive, no longer open about where she was spending much of her time and with whom. She made up stories that weren't believable. She was clearly hiding a big part of her life from me. A wall was going up between us, and it broke my heart. So when I joined the Bible study, Mel stayed away. Her absence gave her another opportunity to do whatever it was that she didn't want me to know about. And at about the time I gave my life to Christ, Mel came out as openly gay. "Let me be who I am!" she once shouted at me.

The rest of the time at the school was really hard. We still loved each other, but felt that we were living our lives poles apart. We applied to different colleges and ended up at different places, Mel at Cornell and I here. Earlier we could not have imagined ever going to separate schools. But here we are. Mel has been in several same-sex relationships since arriving at Cornell.

Our differences are obvious. Mel is gay and I am straight. Mel is not a Christian and I am. Mel is at best indifferent, at worst hostile to my faith in Christ, which is the most precious and life-giving thing to me. I've bent over backwards to try to convince her that my faith is not hostile to her, that Jesus loves her to the point of dying for her, but she's not buying it. "Ah, love the sinner, hate the sin, right? I've heard that one before!" I pray fervently for her every day. I hope that when we are back at the same graduate school in the fall, God will restore our relationship and even more that Mel will fall in love with Jesus as her Savior and Lord.

So for several years now I've been struggling to understand God's mind on the issue of homosexuality. What does the Bible really say about it? I've read the claims and arguments on all sides. How does what we know about homosexuality today, as compared to what was known about it during biblical times, inform our discussion? Why are some people gay? Are they "born gay," as Dave's reference to scientific research seems to suggest? Does that mean that God actually created them that way? Why would God create them gay if being gay is sinful? Why would God "bake in" the sin, to use Amanda's term? What does the idea that homosexuality is "a result of the fall" really mean? In what sense, if any, is it true? Is there really such a thing as "God's design for human gender and sexuality"? If so, how do gay, lesbian, transgender, and intersex people fit into it? Or, if they don't fit, what does that say about their place in God's world? My answers to these questions are provisional, and I am open to other ways of thinking. Having heard all three of you, I find myself still dissatisfied with the proposals we've come up with so far. Most importantly, these questions are not just academic to me. They concentrate on my sister Mel. I long for her to be in the place God would want her to be in living out her true sexual identity, whatever that may look like. I love Melanie with all my heart and know that God loves her infinitely more. I so long for her to find and lose herself in that infinite love.

PHILIP: Steph, I hear your heart. You speak for me as well. That whole menu of questions you've just recited is so my own. Thank you for formulating them so well.

AMANDA: I would love to meet Melanie some day. We have so much in common, and I would love to share with her the story of my release from my same-sex way of life.

DAVID: Thank you, Steph, for your story. Even though neither you nor I have felt same-sex attraction personally, you have been much closer to the heartbreak so often associated with it than I have. I so appreciate your heart for your sister and for all gay people, and the personal dimension as well as the depth of your questions.

STEPHANIE: Thanks guys. I really appreciate that. So here I go. First, I'd like to change our approach to the issue we're discussing. So far, we've been looking at the Bible to try to find out whether the Bible permits or forbids same-sex relationships, including same-sex marriage. We've been looking at a very small set of biblical texts, considering different interpretations of those texts. I'm going to do that as well, since I think doing so is essential to our project. But I believe that project is bigger than that. Here's how I would restate what I believe is our real project: *"Given everything we know about homosexuality today, are we justified or not in claiming that God not only permits but also blesses same-sex relationships built on vows of lifelong mutual faithfulness?"* So I need to begin by defending this way of restating our project. My restatement brings to the surface the following parameters about how we should engage with the Bible in dealing with difficult contemporary questions—this one in particular:

1. In order to arrive at a theologically and ethically sound position on the question of same-sex relationships, we need to draw on all the sources of knowledge available to us.

2. The Bible does not tell us everything we know or need to know about homosexuality.

3. The results of settled scientific research on homosexuality (or any other subject legitimately studied by science) is an aspect of God's continuing revelation of truth about the natural world he has created.

4. In principle, God's revelation of truth in the Bible does not contradict his revelation of truth through science or common human experience. All truth is God's truth, as Dave also affirmed last week.

5. When it *appears* that there is a conflict between what God has revealed in the Bible and what God reveals through ongoing properly conducted scientific research, careful discernment is required to resolve this apparent conflict. Such discernment is fallible, and Christians will not always agree on what the correct resolution is.

6. God's revelation of truth in the Bible is embedded in the cultural contexts of the original writers and audiences, and it is critically important to do our best to familiarize ourselves with those contexts to avoid misinterpreting or misappropriating the biblical texts. There is a "cultural distance" between what was considered acceptable and unacceptable in the ancient cultures of biblical times and what is considered acceptable or unacceptable in our time. Often the biblical authors challenge what was considered acceptable in the cultures of their day, but sometimes (perhaps surprisingly) they do not.

7. There is also what I want to call a "cognitive distance" between what we know today and what the biblical authors knew in their own time. They were not in a position to know all that we now know about the world of nature through scientific inquiry. They bear no blame for this, just as we deserve no credit for knowing what we do today. The Holy Spirit's inspiration of the biblical authors does not extend to imparting to them in their day any factual knowledge of the natural world that would come to light only many centuries later through scientific investigation.

So my approach will implicitly be framed by all of the above parameters. Are you all good with that?

AMANDA: I'm sorry to have to say this, Steph. I'm not on the same page with you at all. I think you are diminishing the authority of the Bible. The Bible is not just one source of truth that needs to be harmonized with others. The truth of the Bible overrides alleged "truth" from any other source. That's because God's word is without error. It does not stand in need of "correction" by any other presumed "authority." The Bible is God's infallible word, whereas science is man's fallible word—pardon me, fallible *human* word. Science seems to be constantly revising its previous conclusions, so how can you possibly assign any authoritative truth to it? Whatever science may tell us about homosexuality today may be "revised away" fifty years from now. Not only that, the Bible is sufficient. It tells us all we need to know. And about homosexuality it tells us two things: one, that homosexuality is sin, contrary to God's design for humanity; and two, that God can forgive and heal homosexuality through the atoning work of Christ and the empowering work of the Holy Spirit.

DAVID: I hear both of you, Steph and Amanda. These are huge issues, which are making a lot of noise and generating a lot of heat within the Christian community, without garnering much consensus. We won't be able to resolve these among the four of us in just one night.

PHILIP: I hear Amanda, too, but I'm more aligned with Stephanie. Amanda's voice reminds me of the kind of absolutism that I encountered in the church of my youth, before I got kicked out. Nothing personal, Amanda, but there's an "either-or" mentality, a "this way or the highway" tone to how you come across that hits me hard in my gut. Sorry.

AMANDA: Sorry also, Phil. I didn't mean to come across that way, believe me. But as I said earlier, attempts to harmonize the Bible with science always tend to end with science on top and the Bible on the bottom. When the authority of the Bible is minimized, its life-changing power is rendered ineffective. That said, I'm fine with hearing Steph out. I probably won't end up agreeing with her, but I'll feel free to comment as we go.

STEPHANIE: Please do, Amanda. Thanks for your feedback just now. I needed to hear that. The whole purpose of engaging in these conversations together is to challenge and be challenged by one another, and let the Holy Spirit speak into our conversations as we listen to each other with humility and openness to criticism. Above all, we are and will remain friends in Christ, regardless of the outcome of our conversations.

AMANDA: I certainly affirm that!

STEPHANIE: I knew you would, Amanda. Okay, I'll begin by sharing my views on the biblical texts we've been talking about, interacting with the views you guys have already expressed. Let me begin with the question about God's design. Phil suggested that God's design for human sexuality includes the multiple minority sexual identities people actually have, and that the Genesis account of the creation of male and female should not be read as "binary," so as to exclude these minorities from God's design. Amanda and Dave disagreed. I side with Amanda and Dave on this point: just because marshes and frogs are presumed to be included in God's creative acts in the prior days of creation, it doesn't follow that minority genders and sexual identities should also be presumed to be included, for the reasons Dave stated last week. I think we have no choice but to acknowledge that homosexuality is not part of God's design, not what God had intended for his original creation of humanity. And so in some sense it is true that same-sex attraction is "a result of the fall."

PHILIP: It sounds again like you are just dismissing the reading that I proposed for God's design in Genesis, Steph, without really refuting it.

STEPHANIE: I don't mean to be dismissive, Phil. But I honestly have to say that I'm not convinced that you've given the more natural interpretation of the Genesis six-day creation account. I agree with Dave's critique of it when he said that it is a stretch to include the creation of other genders and sexual identities as part of God's original design for humanity and that it seemed to him to be "a very contrived way of making the Bible say what you want it to say." Be that as it may, I would like to say something different from all three of you about the foundational text of Genesis 1:27, specifically about the phrase, "male and female he created them." Amanda, you said at our first meeting that this phrase indicates that God created two "and only two" genders, as though the number is somehow important. You also said that you assumed that the male is created with built-in sexual desire for the female, and the female for the male, as though there's an implication for sexuality in the phrase—in fact, you said that this rules out any homosexual desire as being proper to the creation of human beings. And you concluded that homosexual desire, not to mention homosexual behavior, is not in accordance with God's original design for human beings, and therefore sin. That's a lot of mileage out of a single short biblical phrase, don't you think?

AMANDA: Well, isn't all of that implied in the phrase?

STEPHANIE: I'm not sure, Amanda. I'm inclined to think that you could be reading all of that into it. Phil, I took your alternative reading of Genesis 1 as a move against Amanda's position. You called her reading a "Platonic fiction": a heavenly "ideal world" that does not correspond to the earthly reality we actually experience. What did you mean by that?

PHILIP: Amanda's picture of an "ideal" heterosexual maleness and femaleness carries the implication that those of us who don't fit into that ideal somehow fall short—we are less than what God intended us to be; we're failures in some sense. That's deeply hurtful. Sorry if I showed a somewhat cynical tone when I used that phrase.

STEPHANIE: No worries, Phil. So your account of the phrase, read in the context of the six-day creation story that preceded it, was essentially a protest against the exclusivity that you saw in Amanda's account?

PHILIP: Yeah, that was probably the motivation. But that makes my account neither wrong nor right. I'm still thinking about Dave's critique of it last week.

STEPHANIE: Does this mean that you agree with Amanda that probably some statement or other about a "creation design" for humanity relating to gender and sexuality is being made in Genesis 1, but you disagree with her about what that statement is?

PHILIP: I guess so.

STEPHANIE: In that case I'd like to challenge both of you. I don't think this brief phrase, "male and female he created them," is intended at all to have any implication about contemporary questions about sexuality and gender identity. It is worth asking the question why the author of Genesis 1 included that phrase in the creation story, and to look to the context for an answer. And we find the answer in the very next verse. Take a look:

> So God created man in his own image,
>   in the image of God he created him;
>   *male and female he created them.*
>
> And God blessed them. And God said to them, *"Be fruitful and multiply and fill the earth* and subdue it, and have dominion over the fish of the sea and over the birds of the heavens and over every living thing that moves on the earth."

It's clear that the point of the mention of "male and female" is to account for human propagation. There will be no fruitfulness, no multiplication, no filling of the earth without a biological mechanism to make that possible. It takes two people, one who is anatomically male and one who is anatomically female, to reproduce. That's just a stable biological fact and, I'm suggesting, the *only* gender fact intended by the phrase. Neither Amanda's position nor Phil's position is ruled in or ruled out. The "male and female he created them" phrase simply doesn't speak to issues of sexuality and gender identity. Commentators and theologians over the centuries have read these issues into them. So that's my take on Genesis 1.

DAVID: I'll certainly have to think more about that. So what's your take on Genesis 2, the creation of Eve as a "helper fit for" Adam, and their joining in a union of "one flesh"?

STEPHANIE: Is it okay if I punt on that for now, Dave? I'd like to present my views about the exclusion or inclusion of same-sex marriage after we look again at the other passages. If you don't mind, I'll start with the Leviticus prohibition.

DAVID: Okay, let's have it.

STEPHANIE: As Phil said, the section in which the prohibition is embedded is the "Holiness Code." Lots of things are prohibited in this section and many of them are described as abominable. Some prohibitions are dietary, some appear to be concerned with hygiene and ritual cleanliness issues, and some are clearly moral. There are also some that seem simply baffling to a modern reader, and commentators speculate variously what the rationales for these prohibitions might have been. Of what sort is the prohibition against male homosexual acts? Is it a hygiene or cleanliness issue, like the prohibition against having sex with a menstruating woman? Is it a moral issue, like the prohibition against sacrificing one's children to Molech that Amanda mentioned last week? Is it a cultural issue like the one in Phil's example, the prohibition against wearing garments made out of two different materials? Phil thinks it's a cultural issue involving patriarchy, of treating a man (a superior) like a woman (an inferior). Amanda thinks it's a moral issue, a transgression of a divinely created boundary between the two sexes of Genesis 1. As I've just said, I don't agree that Genesis 1 is at all about such a boundary, but that doesn't mean that the writer of Leviticus didn't understand the prohibition that way. As for Phil's suggestion, it's plausible, but no less "speculative" than Amanda's. So I'm not sure whether the prohibition is still in effect today.

DAVID: I've read that a good way to distinguish those Old Testament commands that are no longer in effect today from those that still are is to see if the command is repeated in the New Testament. If it is, it is still in effect today.

STEPHANIE: And if it is not, it is no longer in effect? I don't recall seeing the prohibition against child sacrifice repeated in the New Testament!

DAVID: I didn't say that an Old Testament command not repeated in the New Testament is no longer in effect. What I meant to say is that repetition in the New Testament is a *sufficient* condition for still being in effect, but not a *necessary* condition.

PHILIP: Philosophy scores again, Dave!

STEPHANIE: Okay, I get that. But *is* the prohibition against male homosexual acts actually repeated in the New Testament? I think Phil has raised some legitimate doubts about that—at least against an interpretation of it that applies the prohibition universally, as applicable to everyone. So let me revisit the New Testament passages and give you my take on them.

AMANDA: I would love to hear your take, Steph.

STEPHANIE: Okay. As to the 1 Corinthians and 1 Timothy vice list passages, I don't take a strong view either way on who the "softies" and "male-bedders" are. It could be, as Phil suggested, that these two groups refer to males involved in homosexual prostitution or some other pagan practice involving homosexuality. It could also be that the reference is broader, to include any people engaged in male homosexual activity of any sort, as Amanda thought and Dave was inclined to agree. However, since "male-bedders" is paired with "softies" and "softies" in a sexual context pretty clearly refers to male prostitutes—slaves groomed for sexual service—it seems to me that the scales tip in favor of Phil's account, even if it might also be true that Paul's choice of the term "male bedders" is an invention of his, derived from the Leviticus passages. I agree with Dave's statement that by themselves these texts are not in any way conclusive, so I wouldn't base a position on them either way. But instead of focusing on whether Paul had specific pagan practices in mind or whether he was referring to homosexuality in general, I'd like to focus on what most likely Paul would have thought about these pagan practices. We don't know that apart from looking at what else Paul writes, and the only place he does so is in Romans 1, so I want to take another look at that chapter. More needs to be said about it than what we've said so far.

I agree with Phil's contextual approach: Paul is not giving his readers a general discourse about humanity's lapse into homosexuality. His target is gentile or pagan depravity in chapter 1 and, in chapter 2, Jewish hypocrisy. And he no doubt visualizes, along with his audience, the Roman orgies indulged in by the aristocracy along with other pagan homosexual practices, attributing such depraved behavior directly to their apostasy. I agree also that the "exchange" attributed to these god-forsaken gentiles—their giving up natural sexual relations in exchange for unnatural ones—is or is the result of their active choice, not something passive that just "happened" to them. That said, though, I agree with Amanda and Dave that Paul's declaration in verses 26 and 27 that the gentiles' homosexual depravity is "contrary to nature" is targeted against homosexuality per se, and not just restricted to pagan manifestations of it. I don't agree at all with Phil's reading of the natural-unnatural distinction here.

PHILIP: Ouch, Steph. I feel a scholarly challenge to my interpretation coming on. Go for it, though. This is definitely your territory.

STEPHANIE: Okay, here's what I found in my research for the paper in my "Sex and Sexuality" class. The phrases "contrary to nature," *para phusin* in Greek, along with its twin *kata phusin* ("in accordance with nature") are very common in the surviving Greek philosophical texts. I'm pretty sure Paul and his philosophically educated contemporaries were familiar with these phrases. Aristotle is the Greek philosopher who thought most systematically about the concept of *phusis* or nature. In his view, the nature of a substance, let's say a biological substance—a plant or an animal or a human being—is determined by its type, or species, or form, or essence; for our purposes these can all be considered the same. A particular human being, Socrates, let's say, has a nature that conforms to (or better: just *is*) the nature of a human being, since that's his type or essence: human being. So what is "natural" for Socrates to do is just what is natural for a human being in general to do. If Socrates has behaviors that are not typical of human beings in general, then those behaviors are *unnatural* for Socrates, regardless of what his individual inclinations or proclivities might be. This sense of what is natural was taken over by the Stoics, who situated the concept of nature within their ruling idea of Reason (*Logos*) and recommended a way of life "in conformity with nature" as rational and therefore virtuous. There is every reason to believe that Paul was familiar with Stoic thought. There are distinct traces of it in his theology, and his native city, Tarsus in Cilicia, was the site of a major Stoic school at the time Paul grew up and lived there.

PHILIP: That's very interesting, but what does it prove?

STEPHANIE: I think it proves that Paul uses "natural" in a normative sense. To behave in ways that are "natural" to your species is to behave the way you're supposed to behave; to behave in ways that are "contrary to (your species') nature" is to behave in a way you're not supposed to behave. And I think the idea of a divine "creation order" that is normative for God's creatures is lurking in the background. Notice that when Paul calls out homosexual behavior among both women and men as "contrary to nature," he actually uses the terms "females" and "males," not (as most translations have it), "women" and "men." For a female to have sex with a female is "contrary to (female) nature" and for a male to have sex with a male is "contrary to (male) nature." That suggests that Paul is harkening back to Genesis 1:27, the creation of "male and female." We've looked at this text earlier, and I said that I did not find any implication in it regarding gender roles and boundaries. But I admitted as a possibility that the Levitical prohibition might, as Amanda proposed, be based on such an understanding of that text. Centuries of traditions of rabbinic teaching and commentary might have overlaid that text with this meaning. The same is probably true for the Romans passage.

PHILIP: So what do you take the implications of this for my position to be?

STEPHANIE: If I'm right, Phil, then Paul's objection to the same-sex desires and acts he sees all around him is that they fail to conform to divinely ordained boundaries, and he takes these boundaries to apply universally, not merely relatively to cultures. So I'm not convinced by your alternative interpretation, namely that same-sex acts are unnatural *for straight people*, implying that they are not unnatural *for gay people*. On your interpretation it would be equally unnatural for gay people to engage in heterosexual sex. That was your objection to Amanda's consideration of marriage to Mike, remember? You may be right that such a marriage would be extremely challenging, but it would not be "unnatural" in Paul's use of the term. Even a marriage between Amanda and yourself, which you called "doubly unnatural," would be considered natural by Paul, just because it would be a marriage between a male and a female.

PHILIP: But there are serious problems, aren't there, with Paul's concept of what is and is not "natural"? In 1 Corinthians 11:14–15 he says, "Does not nature (*phusis*) itself teach you that if a man wears long hair it is a disgrace for him, but if a woman has long hair, it is her glory? For her hair is given to her for a covering." Is he kidding? Is a man crossing a gender boundary if he lets his hair grow long and is a woman doing that as well if she cuts hers short? Should we kick people who "violate this divinely ordained boundary" out of our churches? Why can't we just say that Paul's understanding of what is natural and what is not is more culture-bound than he was aware of? Shouldn't we just admit that Paul's appeal to what is natural in Romans 1 reflects his roots in Judaism and Greek philosophy, but is not God's word to us today? Let's have some consistency here!

STEPHANIE: Fair point, Phil. On the surface there is indeed a problem. We don't think that hair length is an issue involving "nature" in any way at all. The idea that there are creational norms for hair length along gender lines strikes us as absurd. Hair length standards, differing from culture to culture, are a matter of convention. So why would Paul seem to suggest otherwise? Some commentators, realizing this, have suggested that by "nature" (*phusis*) in this passage Paul actually *means* "convention." And some of those go on to suggest that if Paul means "convention" here, he must do so as well in Romans 1. His point in Romans 1 would then be that people engaging in homosexual acts are flouting convention! I can't think of anything that is as much of a travesty of biblical exegesis as this is! In Greek thought, "nature" and "convention" are antonyms, not synonyms. There were huge debates in the fifth century BCE, the time of Socrates, around the theme of justice. Are claims to justice based on "nature," *phusis*, some objective standard that reflects how things really are, or are they merely matters of "convention," *nomos*? In Greek thought the concepts of *phusis* and *nomos* are antithetical to each other. The one way these passages actually *cannot* be reconciled is by translating or interpreting *phusis* as "convention"!

PHILIP: So is Paul saying that hair length norms are matters of creation order, divinely ordained and normative?

STEPHANIE: He's not saying anything as loaded as that. He's saying that long hair on a man is a "disgrace," and long hair on a woman is "her glory." These are clearly aesthetic judgments. He's operating with a sense of aesthetic fittingness. It isn't fitting for a man to have his hair long. (How long is too long for a man, we want to know?) Nor is it fitting for a woman to have her hair short. (How short is too short for a woman?) It's a well-known question in the field of aesthetics whether aesthetic judgments are objective or subjective—that is, whether beauty is in the eye of the beholder or somehow inheres in the object beheld. I think the verse shows that Paul would take the latter view, and he expresses it by saying that "nature teaches" that. That expression in this context is just a colloquial, idiomatic manner of speaking, not an application of a philosophically established concept. Isn't it just obvious, he's saying, that long hair looks disgraceful on a man but on a woman it's glorious? (I probably should add that this doesn't mean that Paul's aesthetic objectivism is the right view to take about aesthetic judgments—divine inspiration doesn't guarantee that!)

PHILIP: This sounds a bit dodgy to me, Steph.

STEPHANIE: I don't think it is, but we can disagree about that. All right, I'm ready to go back to Romans 1, because I do want to say more about that important text.

AMANDA: I do want to hear more about it from you, Steph. I heard you agreeing that Paul is saying there that homosexuality is unnatural for any human being. So he's saying that homosexuality is sin, right?

STEPHANIE: That's a huge jump, Amanda. I've noticed you making this jump quite a few times before but I haven't called you on it so far. Let's not put words into the apostle's mouth.

PHILIP: I keep hearing Amanda say it, too. I find that totally disheartening.

STEPHANIE: Dear Phil, take heart. Amanda also reacted several times when she heard things that were hard for her. Our agreement was that we would hear each other out. Besides, this is not the last thing to be said about these verses.

PHILIP: All right. You did say there's more to be said, so please go on.

STEPHANIE: Okay, so from where does Paul get the idea that what is "contrary to (human) nature" is contrary to God's creation order? Paul is not alone among the Jewish writers of his day in making this judgment. For example, a contemporary of his, the great and prolific Jewish philosopher Philo of Alexandria also used the language of "natural" and "unnatural" in his accounts of homosexual sex. By this he appears to have meant that homosexuality is, first, not procreative and, second, contrary to the way God has created human beings. He is very likely thinking about particular Old Testament texts such as the Genesis and Leviticus texts; he certainly grounds his thinking in the idea of a divine creation order for human beings.

PHILIP: Sounds Platonic.

STEPHANIE: Exactly right, Phil. Philo was a great philosopher who interpreted the biblical doctrine of creation through a Platonic lens. He was not the last to do so. St. Augustine also followed that interpretive strategy in his commentaries and sermons on Genesis. There are profound insights to be gained that way, but also deep pitfalls to be avoided.

AMANDA: So do you think that this is what Paul would also have meant by his declaration of homosexuality as "unnatural"?

STEPHANIE: I do think it's likely, Amanda. I do think Paul believes that God *designed* human beings to be heterosexual. Furthermore—and this is a different but hugely important point—I think Paul believes that God *actually creates* each human being as heterosexual.

AMANDA: And you don't agree?

STEPHANIE: Let me sidestep that question for now, Amanda. I'll get to it after we cover some more territory first.

AMANDA: Didn't you say a bit earlier that you didn't believe in a "creation order" for human beings?

STEPHANIE: No, I didn't say that. What I said was that the phrase in Genesis 1:27, "male and female he created them," interpreted in context, doesn't refer to a "creation order" for human gender and sexuality. I didn't say that I didn't believe in such a creation order or, as I prefer to put it, a divine design. Actually I do believe in it, but not on the basis of this particular verse. I believe in it on the testimony of Scripture taken as a whole, and of my own experience of God's beautiful world.

AMANDA: Can you explain that?

STEPHANIE: The world that God has created, the world that I live in and am a part of, is an orderly and beautiful place, fully "charged with the grandeur of God." I am impressed by how exquisitely things fit together. The world that I observe is brimming with teleology—with purposiveness. The human body and those of other animals are works of art. And we keep advancing in our knowledge of the teleology of the human body. The decoding of the human genome in the 1990s is a spectacular example.

DAVID: Philosophers and theologians have attempted to construct "proofs" of the existence of God on the basis of such observations of teleology. I've studied a number of them and find them quite convincing.

STEPHANIE: My own sense of God's reality to which the teleology of nature bears witness is not based on a conclusion inferred from premises, but from an immediate experience of it. Yes, there is definitely a magnificent "divine design" to creation! And this design includes the creation of human (and animal) males and females. It is obvious to me that the reproductive organs and systems of males and females are made for each other, that reproduction is advanced by innate sexual drives of males and females to mate with each other, drives to raise and protect their young, and so on. And all of this strikes me with a deep sense of "fittingness." That's the way it's supposed to be! It often draws out of me an overwhelming impulse to praise and worship the God who devised it all!

DAVID: Yes, there are a number of psalms that celebrate this. "Let the whole creation praise the Lord"; "let the glory of the Lord fill the earth," and so on. God's answer to Job in chapter 38 of that book highlights it too.

STEPHANIE: But then there are also plenty of instances where some of these biological structures and mechanisms have gone awry and fail to function properly—instances of "dysteleology," one might call them. For example, there are people whose auditory systems from the moment of birth don't work right. They are born deaf. Others are born blind. A chromosomal failure results in children being born with Down syndrome. When we encounter these instances, we are struck with a sense of the unfittingness of that: this is *not* the way things are supposed to be. We respond with compassion and adjust our expectations. We do not require people who have such impairments to behave in ways that we would expect of people without these impairments. We do our best to minimize the effects of these limitations and help the people who have them to live lives as close to "normal" as possible.

PHILIP: I think I see where you're going with this. Are you saying that homosexuality is a disability? An instance of—what did you call it, "dysteleology"? Are gay people broken? Is that what you're saying? If it is, you probably should know that back in 1973 the American Psychiatric Association removed homosexuality from its list of psychiatric disorders. "Homosexuality per se," they said, "should no longer be considered a 'psychiatric disorder.'"

STEPHANIE: But they also added, "It should be defined instead as a 'sexual orientation disturbance.'" That phrase is their acknowledgment that being gay is not the way sexual orientation is supposed to be. Still, I can understand your rising frustration, Phil. Just as I could understand Amanda's earlier. I hope we can hear each other out. Let me go on for a bit. Theologically I try to make sense of these dissonant "not the way it's supposed to be" instances within the larger structure of "the way it's supposed to be" by applying a fourfold distinction I find often made by many theologians I respect: "creation, fall, redemption and restoration."

DAVID: Yes, I've also read about that quartet. The Bible has been described as the "story" of God's plan for his creation. In this analysis "creation" refers to God's design, God's original intent for the world he created. In the Bible this is told as a narrative in Genesis 1 and 2, and as I said it is celebrated in some of the psalms. The "fall" refers to the damage done to the world by the entrance of sin and its effects. The narrative for this is in Genesis 3 and its immediate aftermath in the succeeding chapters, through chapter 11. "Redemption" refers to God's plan to undo that damage, beginning with the call and promises to Abraham in chapter 12. Almost the whole of the rest of the Bible is the story of the execution of that plan, climaxing in the death of Jesus on the cross and his victorious resurrection, and going forward to and beyond our own day. We live in the time when the effects of the fall are still very much with us, but we already witness signs of the transformational power of redemption through the lives changed by the proclamation of the gospel and the impact of those lives upon society. Finally, "restoration" refers to the complete elimination of all the damaging effects of the fall through the renewal of the whole of creation. The biblical chapters that describe this still-future scenario in a visionary way are chapters 21 and 22 of the book of Revelation. This "restoration" is the renewal of God's creation where all things, including all of redeemed humanity, will be eternally reconciled to God.

STEPHANIE: A great summary, Dave.

AMANDA: So how do you apply this to our issue?

STEPHANIE: A moment ago you questioned whether I believe in a "creation order" for sexuality and gender identity. Yes, I do. It's the first of this foursome. I do believe in a divine design for human gender and sexuality. God's original plan for humanity (and many non-human animal species) is that they should be able to reproduce and form and enhance bonds of affection for each other. So he created them male and female. Sex in this plan would have the dual function of accomplishing both. But then the fall occurred.

PHILIP: I was right. Like Dave and Amanda you believe that "homosexuality is a result of the fall." Your account of the "creation order" is pretty much the same as theirs. I'm disappointed, Steph. I had hoped for something different from you.

STEPHANIE: Hold on, Phil. That's only part of it. Now's the time to bring to our table front and center the question that has popped up several times now: *Does God create people gay?* What does each of you think?

AMANDA: It's pretty obvious to me that you've answered your own question, Steph. If homosexuality is a result of the fall and if it has no place in God's creation order, the answer is obviously negative. God creates people straight, not gay. Their being gay is a manifestation of sin, obviously. Don't you think so too, Dave?

DAVID: I'm not sure. I agree that being gay is an effect of sin, but doubt that it is sinful in itself. On the question whether God *actually creates* people gay I'm very uncertain, and I'd like to hear more about this from Stephanie.

Philip: I disagree with Amanda. As I've said before, I believe that God does create people gay, that Amanda and I are gay because God created us that way. You may not agree with my account of Genesis 1, but somehow we have a place within God's design. So what's your own answer to your question, Steph?

Stephanie: Okay, time to put my next card on the table: I believe that God does indeed create people gay, even if being gay is an effect of the fall and not part of God's original design.

David: That seems very counterintuitive, Steph, even paradoxical, if not downright contradictory. Do you have any support from the Bible for claiming that?

Stephanie: As a matter of fact I do, Dave. A significant turning point in my thinking came when I seriously faced that question head on. I think most of the people who would answer this question affirmatively probably think like you do, Phil. In their view God's creation design for human gender and sexuality includes the variety of sexual and gender identities that we see around us. I've already said in response to your account why, as an interpretation of Genesis, I think that is implausible. But I do affirm, perhaps surprisingly, that it is God who makes people gay. I don't believe, as Amanda does, that if God makes them that way he makes them with "sin baked in." But I do believe that God makes people—and that includes all of us, as I'll try to show you—with some fall-induced condition or other, none of which are instances of "sin baked in."

David: You're getting mysterious on me, Steph. Can you explain that?

Stephanie: Yes. Some years ago I was in a Bible study, and we were studying God's call to Moses in Exodus. Out of the burning bush God calls Moses to confront the Pharaoh and command this Egyptian sovereign to "let my people go." Moses protests that he is not qualified to take that role. He has a speech issue (so he says) and begs to be excused. This is how his exchange with Yahweh goes (Exodus 4:10-11):

> But Moses said to the Lord, "Oh, my Lord, I am not eloquent, either in the past or since you have spoken to your servant, but I am slow of speech and of tongue." Then the Lord said to him, *"Who*

has made man's mouth? Who makes him mute, or deaf, or seeing, or
blind? Is it not I, the Lord?"

I was stunned when I read this. Here is God telling Moses that it is *he*
himself who makes people with the impairments they have—impairments
they would not have had if the world had not fallen from its original creation design. "Mute, deaf, blind . . ."

AMANDA: Okay, you're saying that God creates people with the impairments they have. But surely you're not suggesting that being same-sex
attracted is merely some kind of handicap that some people are born with?

PHILIP: *Merely* a handicap? Why should we think about being gay as
a "handicap" at all?

STEPHANIE: Hold it, you two! I didn't use the word "handicap." We
need to be very careful with the language that we use. I wouldn't say that
being gay is a handicap. Gay people are able to function very well and pretty
independently in the world (unless, besides being gay, they happen also
to be blind or deaf, etc.). Special ADA-approved accommodations for gay
people are not needed. So words like "handicap" and "disability" don't fit.
I've described it as an impairment, the result of a malfunction. Something
in their system isn't functioning properly. Handicaps will involve impairments, but impairments by themselves aren't handicaps.

DAVID: Your phrase "not functioning properly" reminds me of an idea
developed by a stellar Christian philosopher whom I greatly admire. This
philosopher argued that our cognitive capacities (the capacities we have
to form beliefs) may or may not function properly, and that their proper
functioning is defined by reference to a "design plan" for such capacities.
And in biology the idea that the parts and systems of living organisms have
functions has made a comeback, despite the fact that the idea of purpose in
nature as a category of scientific explanation was rejected in early modern
philosophy and science. What you are saying is that with gay people there
is a lack of conformity between God's *design plan* for human sexuality and
the way God *actually creates* them.

STEPHANIE: That's an excellent way of stating my position, Dave. In
conversations about how God "creates" people, there is often an ambiguity

that we should be aware of. We need to make sure that we're not equivocating on this term. On the one hand, we might be referring to God's pre-fall design plan—what is regularly referred to as the "creation order" for human gender and sexuality—or, on the other hand, we might be referring to the way God actually brings individual people into being. When I raise the question of whether God "creates" some people gay, I'm taking it in the latter sense, not the former. So I'll reserve the term "create" for that latter sense, and use the term "design" for the former. I want to say that there's a gap between God's universal design for human beings and the way God sometimes creates actual individual human beings. And the existence of that gap is accounted for by the fall.

DAVID: Wait a minute, Steph. Are you saying that when, in the Exodus passage you cited, God says that he "makes" people mute, deaf or blind, he actually *causes* in the sense that he *intends* them to be afflicted with these effects of the fall? That sounds very implausible given the character and purposes of God as revealed in Scripture as a whole.

STEPHANIE: I'm not saying that, Dave. Theologians have long struggled with the "problem of evil," the problem of reconciling the manifestations of sin and evil in the world with the sovereign power and infinite goodness and wisdom of God. There is a theological tradition that claims that God decreed the fall and its effects from eternity as part of his plan for creating the world. From that perspective God does indeed ordain all the effects of the fall, including the impairments that people are actually born with. People who hold this perspective have no trouble with the idea that God "makes" or "causes" people to be blind or deaf or impaired in some other way. The opposite perspective seems to suggest that the fall and its effects are neither caused nor intended by God, but are simply permitted by God. I'm inclined to take a middle position: God is not the direct cause of these effects, nor does he intend them per se; nevertheless, they are within his providential sovereign purpose and control. But saying that God merely "permits" these effects seems to be too weak; it seems too passive. It makes God a bystander. The best word I can come up with to capture a sense weaker than "intending" but stronger than "permitting" is "authorizing." God does not intend these effects, nor does he merely permit them, but he does put his signature on them. The use of the verb "makes" in this verse, followed by the rhetorical question, "Is it not I, the Lord?" suggests that

God takes full responsibility for them. God uses these effects to serve his purposes, so that they are redeemed. We cannot always tell how they are redeemed, and often they seem irredeemable to us, but that's because we can't see the whole picture. Following the Exodus passage I'm willing to say that God "makes" or "creates" people with the congenital impairments they have, provided that we understand that "making" in the nuanced way I've just described.

DAVID: So are you saying that it is part of God's *plan* for Amanda's life and Phil's to be same-sex attracted?

STEPHANIE: Again, Dave, we need to be more nuanced. It is not part of God's "pre-fall" plan for anyone's life, but it is part of his "post-fall" plan for some people's lives. Given the fall, God adapts his various plans for our individual lives to the reality of the fall and its effects. And so God authorizes whatever congenital impairments we happen to have and creates us in conformity with that authorization. These impairments are not divine mistakes. They are always meant to be redemptive, even if we can't always see how.

DAVID: I'm not comfortable with the claim that God "creates" people that way, Steph, or even that God "authorizes" the impairments and incorporates them into his post-fall plan for their lives. Even with your nuanced account, it still sounds too much like God is the cause of, and intends, the various effects of the fall to occur. And your appeal to this one verse in the Bible sounds a little suspicious to me. It's like you're already committed to your position and have serendipitously happened upon a proof text to support it.

STEPHANIE: I could come up with plenty of other Scriptures that suggest that God authorizes many of the fall's effects, not only human biological impairments. In any case, Dave, how would *you* account theologically (as opposed to medically or scientifically) for people who are born with a liability to manifest these impairments? If this is not within God's plan for their lives and the impairments aren't the results of choices or environmental circumstances, what's the explanation? Chance? Bad luck? Satanic malfeasance? What would *that* say about God's sovereignty?

DAVID: Here's another problem I have with your view, Steph. If we tell people who are gay but not yet believers in Jesus that God made them that way, won't they feel resentment toward God and turn away from the gospel message? What will they think about the character of God? Isn't the idea that God "authorizes" this impairment—if that's what it is—inconsistent with what the Bible reveals about the character of God? It's hard to avoid the conclusion that God in some sense *wants* them to be gay.

STEPHANIE: I hear that, Dave. It's probably not the first thing we'll want to tell our gay friends who are seekers. But that doesn't mean it isn't true. We do not know why God authorizes any particular distribution of the natural effects of the fall among his fallen human creatures. All we know is that this is within the scope of his loving providence, and that he intends it for their good. God calls us to trust in his wisdom, even when we cannot understand it.

DAVID: Hmm. I'd like to think that that's true, but I'm not really sure.

PHILIP: For my part Steph, I'm not really sure I'm ready to sign on to your view that homosexuality *is* an impairment and not part of God's original design in creation for some of us, as I've argued. But I do agree that *if* you're right about that (and that's a huge "if"), this text in Exodus is encouraging to gay Christians like myself. Either way, it allows us to affirm our sexual orientation as part of God's plan for our lives, however much we might have wanted it to be different. To me, the affirmation that I am gay because God created me that way is comforting and encouraging, not threatening—though I can see how it might be upsetting to someone who doesn't have a relationship with God.

AMANDA: Hold on, everyone! I think we'd agree that there's nothing sinful about being blind, deaf, or mute, wouldn't we? Stephanie, are you suggesting that there's nothing sinful about being gay? That seems totally out of sync with how the Bible consistently talks about homosexuality.

DAVID: Amanda? Haven't we been here before? There's nothing sinful about *being* gay, just *acting* that way.

STEPHANIE: We haven't actually resolved yet whether it is sinful "to act that way," Dave. I still need to come to that. Amanda has a point, though, if you'll recall our discussion about whether Romans 1 excuses same-sex attraction. I agreed with her against you that the passage doesn't excuse it—at least as far as Paul's knowledge and experience of the pagan practices are concerned. But I actually do agree with you, Dave, against Amanda, that having an inborn same-sex orientation is not sinful, even if it is out of conformity with God's design. I do not agree with her idea that if God creates some people with same-sex attractions, then he creates them with "sin baked in."

AMANDA: Are you telling me that you disagree with the Bible, Stephanie? That the Bible is wrong in something that it teaches?

STEPHANIE: We are getting way ahead of ourselves, Amanda. I promise you, we'll get there.

PHILIP: Just a minute ago you said that God has a redemptive purpose for creating us with our various disabilities and impairments. Do you have any such purpose to suggest?

STEPHANIE: Not a particular purpose for every particular case. But I do have a suggestion. In the New Testament story of Jesus healing a man blind from birth, Jesus's disciples raise the question about the cause of the man's congenital blindness (John 9:1–3):

> As he passed by, he saw a man blind from birth. And his disciples asked him, "Rabbi, *who sinned, this man or his parents, that he was born blind?*" Jesus answered, *"It was not that this man sinned, or his parents, but that the works of God might be displayed in him. "*

I think we can universalize this. God creates us, not as exact copies of his design ideal, but as individuals variously marked by the effects of the fall, so that his (redemptive!) works might be displayed in us. This is true for those he creates deaf, mute, blind, and, I suggest, also for those like Amanda and Phil whom he creates gay! And the reason is that the works of God might be displayed in us, whether through our straightness or our gayness.

DAVID: Wow! I've never looked at it that way before.

STEPHANIE: To clarify this I'd like to take a page out of your play-book, Phil, when you gave your account of what Paul meant by "natural" in Romans 1. As I said, I don't agree with your interpretation of "nature" in that passage, but the idea you advanced there, that people have inborn individual sexual natures, gay or straight, is one I'd like to borrow. All of us have two types of nature when it comes to our sexuality. One I shall call our "design nature" or simply "d-nature" to refer to the sexual nature we have in God's *design* for our sexuality. That's the nature Paul is talking about in Romans. That nature is the one we share with all human beings: God designs us all for heterosexuality. But God does not *create* all of us individually straight. Dave and I were created straight, but Amanda and Phil were created gay. Some people are created intersex. I'll call the sexual natures we actually have—because God created us (in the nuanced sense I've described) to have them—our "created nature," or "c-nature" for short.

AMANDA: Stop right there, Steph. Where in the Bible does it say that God creates some of us with sexual natures that deviate from his design?

STEPHANIE: Well, is it God's design for anyone to be blind or mute or deaf? And yet the Bible says that God makes some of us that way. In those cases people's d-natures are to be seeing, hearing, and speaking, and yet God does not create them in conformity with their d-natures. Why, we do not know; as I said, the best we can do is to attribute this to the effect of the fall. That's as far as theological explanation can take us. But there might be scientific explanations. The causes of congenital blindness, deafness, and muteness are ongoing subjects of scientific investigation. So also with the causes of homosexuality, as we've said before. Remember that last week Dave elaborated on the concept of *sexual orientation*, suggesting that a homosexual orientation has, at least in most if not all cases, a neuro-biological origin, and hence that most, if not all, gay people have such an orientation hardwired into their brains from birth. Typically, this orienta-tion is neither chosen nor the result of environmental factors. Like Dave, I take the scientific research on homosexual orientation (in most cases) as having a neurobiological origin—what I've called a neurobiological mal-function—seriously and beyond dispute. Gay people do not choose to be gay. They discover at a certain point in their lives that they are gay. They cannot choose to become straight, even if they wanted to.

David: This reminds me of a candidate for U.S. president in the 2020 election, an openly gay man who said during his campaign, "I would have done anything to not be gay. If you had offered me a pill to make me straight, I would have swallowed it before I could get a sip of water."

Philip: As I recall, he also said to someone who had an issue with his being gay, "If you have a problem with who I am, your problem is not with me. Your quarrel, sir, is with my Creator." The candidate is a committed Christian who owns the way God created him, despite the fact that he wishes God had created him differently. But let me go back to your idea of "impairment," Steph. You said homosexuality is an impairment, though not a handicap or disability. What did you mean by that distinction?

Stephanie: Well, apart from the dysteleology itself, there is the fact that gay couples are limited in not being able to procreate by themselves. They can't both be the natural parents of any children they might want to have.

Philip: If that's a limitation, it can be easily remedied by adoption, as I've already suggested. What other limitations are there? How does the "impairment" limit us? Somehow I can't escape the feeling that you and Dave—even Amanda, for that matter—think that Amanda and I are damaged goods. She may think so, but all you're doing, Steph, is depressing me about my sexuality—of which I've had a lifetime already. We're different, all right, but we're not broken. If Amanda thought you crossed a line for her earlier, I have to tell you that this does the same for me.

Amanda: "Not broken, just different" is a phrase that I'm sure both of us have encountered a lot, Phil. You appear to accept it, but I absolutely agree with Steph that your and my sexual desires are not aligned with the way God designed them to be. We shouldn't pretend that they are. The sooner we accept that fact about ourselves, the better. If you don't mind my saying so, your account of God's design in Genesis as inclusive of minority sexual identities seems to me to be motivated by the "not broken, just different" theme. Nobody wants to think of themselves as broken! I get that. And no Christian wants to be on the outside of God's design. I get that, too. And it would be the height of rudeness and insensitivity for some straight person to wag their finger at you and me and tell us that we're broken! But don't you also believe, Phil, deep down, that your and my sexual attractions are not the way they're supposed to be?

STEPHANIE: If it's any comfort, we're all of us broken. Not a single one of us has every aspect of our lives—biological, psychological, mental, emotional, spiritual—functioning properly and unimpaired. Take myself, for example. As you can see from my thick glasses, I'm very nearsighted. When I was in fourth grade I "came out" to my parents. I told them I couldn't see the board from where I was sitting in the classroom. This was not some deep dark secret that I had kept from them for months, agonizing if they would still love me if they found out. They were not shocked when they heard this, wondering what their friends would think about them having a nearsighted child. In fact, given that they both are nearsighted also, they had actually expected it. We went to the optometrist, I got my eyesight tested and was soon proudly sporting my first pair of glasses! No big deal, right? My point is that my nearsightedness and Amanda's and Phil's gayness are both biological impairments, even though they aren't anywhere nearly as significant for how we navigate our lives. Neither my eyesight nor their sexuality, are "the way they're supposed to be." Just as I have no reason to be ashamed of my eyesight, Amanda and Phil have no reason to be ashamed of their sexuality. Just as it would be crazy for anyone to shame me for my nearsightedness (and no one does), so it is crazy for anyone to shame Amanda and Phil for their sexuality (though plenty of people do).

PHILIP: I'm sorry, Amanda and Stephanie, I can't go there with you. I know I have my share of the sort of biological malfunctions or impairments you're talking about. Like you, Steph, I'm also nearsighted. I also suffer from bouts with Crohn's Disease. And my family medical history, at least on the male side, is one with heart problems. None of my known male ancestors on my father's side has lived beyond the age of sixty-five. I do see those as impairments, not part of God's design. I just don't see being gay that way. That's why I've insisted on a more inclusive interpretation of God's design— which, by the way, I continue to think you and Dave are just dismissing out of hand, without really refuting it. From my perspective the "binary" view of God's design for human gender and sexuality all three of you endorse seems impoverished and reductive. Gay people aren't suffering from any impairment in being gay. Gay (or "queer") people, more than the average population, have a heightened aesthetic sense. They are overrepresented, one might say, in artistic achievements: in design, theater, and, as in my case, music. It could be that whatever it is that makes people gay also makes us exceptionally gifted in the arts. You've heard of the TV series *Queer Eye*, haven't you? Should we say that such giftedness is an impairment?

DAVID: I love that series. I enjoy the banter as much as the creative solutions the team comes up with each week.

PHILIP: Here's what I really want to say. When, a few years ago, I encountered the inclusive interpretation of the Genesis account of God's design and it really entered my soul, so to speak, I cried tears of relief, tears of joy. I was not a mistake! God had planned for the likes of me from the beginning of creation! A huge burden was lifted from my shoulders. Can you believe it? *I am okay just the way I am!* No mistake was made when I was created! People, even my fellow Christians, might not affirm me, but I know God affirms me! And I know that that's all that counts! I am free to enter into the fullness of the life God has for me, including getting married to James! Praise the Lord! The liberation I experienced validated for me the interpretations of the other biblical texts I gave two weeks ago. I am no longer sad or distressed about being gay. I *am* sad and distressed about the continuing exclusion and disapproval I must suffer at the hands of my fellow Christians. For some reason the secular world gets it, but my brothers and sisters in Christ for the most part don't.

STEPHANIE: *(after a long pause, tears in her eyes)* Dearest Phil, I know you are not a mistake. God created you as you are, and he doesn't make mistakes. You have every right to seize on God's affirmation of your life, just the way it is. I join you in lamenting the exclusion you continue to suffer at the hands of many of our fellow Christians. The disagreement that you and I have concerns the meaning of a handful of biblical texts. Like David and Amanda, I just don't see how the phrase "male and female he created them" in Genesis 1:27 can be stretched to fit multiple sexual identities within its scope. Unlike all three of you, I just don't see this text speaking to contemporary questions of gender and sexuality at all. On the one hand, I'm glad that your way of taking this text brought comfort and encouragement to your soul. On the other hand, I'm very wary of taking this or any other text in a way that lies beyond its original intent.

DAVID: There's an important contemporary philosophical issue lurking behind your disagreement, Phil and Steph. This is the question, "What is the meaning of a given text?" Is there an "objective" meaning that the text carries in itself, given to it by its author, or is any meaning it is presumed to have given to it by its readers (and thus is "subjective")? Some, like Stephanie, look for the meaning intended by the author (or artist, since works of art can also be considered texts). To discover this meaning we need to study the author's original language, culture, and socio-political context. That's as close to an "objective" meaning as we can hope to get.

STEPHANIE: Yes, as a classicist, that's what I'm trained to do in studying the texts: to study the languages and the worlds of Herodotus, or Plato, or Cicero. We cannot just invest these texts with our contemporary sensibilities, or else our understandings of them will be distorted. Like these classical texts, the Bible is a set of ancient documents, and it is important to ferret out the original meanings of the authors as closely as we can, especially since we believe those texts to communicate God's very Word to us.

DAVID: On the other hand, there are those who look to the text to speak to our contemporary situation, which may well be different from that of the original authors. On this view, texts are living documents that continue to speak meaningfully across vast stretches of space and time. I think that Phil came to see in the Genesis text an inclusive interpretation that resonated deeply with him in his personal situation and liberated him in the way he's just described.

AMANDA: Doesn't this difference in approaches to "the meaning of the text" also come out in peoples' different appeals to founding legal documents such as the U.S. Constitution? On the one hand you have the approach that appeals to the meaning of "the founders" as the objective meaning of the Constitution and thus having authority. Justices and judges who take that approach are often described as "textualists" or "originalists," and they hold to a more conservative legal philosophy. On the other hand, there is the approach that appeals to what the application of constitutional principles calls for in contemporary situations, which might be very different from the situations the founders found themselves in. The meaning of the Constitution is then defined by the contingencies of our contemporary situation. Justices and judges who favor this approach hold to a more liberal legal philosophy.

STEPHANIE: You're both right, Dave and Amanda. As I've said, my approach to the biblical texts is more like the former approach. I would characterize Phil's approach as more like the latter. What do you think, Phil?

PHILIP: Yes, I would agree. I can't pretend that my inclusive interpretation is right there, word for word in the text. But I do claim to have heard God speaking to me *through* this interpretation and bringing encouragement and deliverance to my soul.

STEPHANIE: I can well imagine you claiming that, Phil. But in determining the meaning of the creation account I do have to go with the "word for word in the text" approach and I'm not seeing inclusivity. I respect your claim, just as Dave respected Amanda's claim three weeks ago, to have heard directly from God; but I'm skeptical just as he was then. I hope that doesn't upset you.

PHILIP: No, I'm not upset. As I've said before, we should all cut each other some slack.

STEPHANIE: Let's just leave it there then. I'll continue my account in terms of homosexuality being a dysteleological impairment of human sexual capacities. As I've said, I stand with you in your lament over your exclusion, and maybe what I have to say in the rest of my "case" for my position will help to make that clearer. Maybe in the end I might even persuade you.

(*To the group*) So when Phil presented his inclusive view of God's design in Genesis, he suggested that the variety of sexual identities in our world should be regarded as on a par with the variety of racial and ethnic groups that populate our planet. Also, being gay, he suggested, is on a par with being left-handed: just as there is nothing "wrong" with being left-handed, so there is nothing "wrong" with being gay. I have to disagree on both counts. I totally agree that there is nothing "impaired" about being white, or black, or Asian, or any other racial group. Racial diversity is indeed to be celebrated. It enriches our world and our experience of being human. I also totally agree that being left-handed is not an impairment of any type. Let me suggest another analogue. Think about albinism, which occurs in all races. Albinos lack a characteristic that their non-albino counterparts do not lack: sufficient pigmentation in their skin to avoid injury by exposure to the sun. So yes, there's something "not the way it's supposed to be" in their dermatological make-up. God's creation design for humanity does not contain myopia or cardiac weakness, nor does it contain albinism. Nor, I'm suggesting, does it contain homosexuality. These are all "effects of the fall," and they all impose some kind of limitation on our lives.

But in what sense are these all "effects of the fall"? I think it's helpful to distinguish two types of effects of the fall: *moral* effects and *natural* effects. The moral effects of the fall can be summed up as "original sin" and the effects of such sin upon our inner lives. This is the story of Adam and Eve's rebellion in the garden of Eden: their willful choice to disobey God brought with it the corruption of the human heart, for them and all subsequent humanity. All of us come into the world with a predisposition to sin, and all of us may be delivered from that predisposition only by the grace of God in Christ. The natural effects of the fall, by contrast, are not the result of any choice of ours. These include any congenital physical ailments we may have or predispositions to diseases or disabilities. These we did not bring upon ourselves by our choices. My and Phil's myopia and Amanda's and Phil's same-sex attractions come under that heading. I'm sure Dave could come up with one or more of his own.

DAVID: Well, for one, I've had asthma since childhood. I have to take medications daily and have to have a rescue inhaler with me at all times. And my brother Greg is autistic.

STEPHANIE: All of these are among the natural effects of the fall. They are not in God's original pre-fall design plan for our lives. They are all the same *type* of affliction, though some have much greater implications for how we live our lives than others. All are associated with sin in the sense that if sin had not entered the world through our first parents' choice, we would not experience them. But we are not deserving of blame for having them. Phil and I do not deserve blame for being myopic. Dave does not deserve blame for being asthmatic, and his brother doesn't deserve blame for being autistic. Albinos do not deserve blame for being under-pigmented. And Amanda and Phil do not deserve blame for being same-sex attracted.

Amanda: I get your distinction between natural and moral effects of the fall, but I don't agree that same-sex desires are among the natural, and not the moral, effects. The desire for something sinful is itself sinful, as I've said several times before. In contrast to the Pharisees who focused on external behavior, Jesus taught that evil actions flow forth from evil desires "of the heart." So if homosexual behavior is sinful, as I believe the Bible clearly teaches it is, then, as I've said before, the desire for such behavior is sinful as well, even if Phil and I can't help having those desires. I also can't help having desires for putting my own interests above those of others, for ignoring God's will and following my own, for wanting to show myself in a good light to others, for excusing my bad behavior, and so on. These desires are manifestations of my sinful nature, my "flesh," against which I am called to wage war. Same with my same-sex desires.

Stephanie: I agree that all the "fleshly" desires you've mentioned are moral effects of the fall. I disagree, though, that same-sex desires fall in the same category. I want to bracket for now your claim that homosexual behavior is sinful. We'll come back to that later. At the moment I want to draw a distinction between desires that manifest the "sinful nature" of our hearts and desires that have a physiological basis in the neurological or biochemical condition of our bodies.

David: It sounds as if you might be suggesting a kind of "mind-body dualism," where the mind or soul has its set of desires, and the body a different set. Plato suggested something like that in the *Republic*.

Stephanie: I'm not sure how my point maps onto the distinction between mind and body, and even less sure how to address the mind-body problem. I do Greek and Latin, Dave. You're the philosopher. I hope my point doesn't depend on us getting totally clear on that problem. That point is simply that we have a whole bunch of physiological desires that are morally neutral: for example, the desire to eat when we are hungry, drink when we are thirsty, to scratch where we itch and, I would add, the desire to seek sexual satisfaction. These desires can function properly or they can malfunction. To feel hungry even when you are full is a malfunction of the desire to eat. To feel an itch on an amputated limb is a malfunction of the desire to scratch. Analogously, to feel sexual attraction to someone of your own gender is a malfunction of the desire for sexual satisfaction. These are all physiological desires malfunctioning, and when they do so they result in impairments of various sorts. They are not expressions of the morally corrupt state of the soul.

AMANDA: It still sounds like you are excusing the inexcusable, Steph. Again, the Bible does not support a distinction between "moral" and "natural" effects of the fall, even if such a distinction seems reasonable to us. We are not to "let sin reign in our mortal bodies," says Paul. He does not separate sins of the soul from sins of the body.

STEPHANIE: Amanda, I'm not making a distinction between sins of the soul and sins of the body. I'm talking about two different kinds of effects of the fall. The moral effects we are responsible for, and need to repent of, while the natural effects we are unable to change but can adapt ourselves to in varying degrees. So I do associate being same-sex-attracted with the fall, but only as a natural effect, not a moral one. Many people like yourself, Amanda—at least in our first conversation three weeks ago—take Romans 1 to teach that homosexuality in general, not just the perverted Greco-Roman practices, is a moral consequence of the fall. That's a mistake, as you yourself were open to admitting two weeks ago. However, another passage in Romans provides the correct connection between our improperly functioning bodies and the fall. This is Romans 8:18–23. Paul brings the fall into his discussion in a way that does involve homosexuality—and albinism, myopia, asthma and autism:

> For I consider that the sufferings of this present time are not worth comparing with the glory that is to be revealed to us. For *the creation waits with eager longing* for the revealing of the sons of God. For *the creation was subjected to futility*, not willingly, but because of him who subjected it, in hope that *the creation itself will be set free from its bondage to corruption* and obtain the freedom of the glory of the children of God. For we know that *the whole creation has been groaning together in the pains of childbirth until now*. And not only the creation, but we ourselves, who have the first-fruits of the Spirit, groan inwardly *as we wait eagerly for* adoption as sons, *the redemption of our bodies*.

DAVID: I see where you're going with this. The creation's subjection to futility, its groaning and longing to be set free—which will happen one day when its redemption is complete and its restoration begins—is today's reality. That reality impinges on all of us in significant ways and will continue to do so for the rest of our mortal lives. We all await "the redemption of our bodies" from all of the ways they malfunction now. As theologians like to say, we live "between the times," the "already" accomplished by Christ's victory on the cross, and the "not yet" when he makes all things new at the end of the age.

STEPHANIE: Correct, Dave. In terms of my distinction between our common d-nature and our various c-natures, the impairments that characterize our c-natures are natural effects of the fall, but nothing like "sin baked in." We will carry these effects in our mortal bodies until the day we die, but they will be absent from our glorious resurrected bodies. In our final state of "restoration," nobody will be nearsighted, asthmatic, autistic—or gay.

DAVID: Jesus taught that in that final state there will be no marriage. So what would the point of gender and sexuality be then?

STEPHANIE: These are mysteries, surely. On the one hand we will have glorified bodies. That leads me to think that we will have these bodies, sex organs and all, in some imperishable form. On the other hand, of what use will sex organs be in a state where there is no sex? Or will there be sex? I can't let myself go there.

AMANDA: Steph, you still haven't answered my question about how you square all this with Scripture, particularly with Romans 1. I see no acknowledgment there of a distinction between a common human d-nature and various individual c-natures, especially homosexual c-natures that people like Phil and myself supposedly have. I hope you won't take this personally, but it sounds like a fancy way to circumvent the obvious.

STEPHANIE: Which is?

AMANDA: That homosexuality, both desires and behavior, violates our God-created nature—our "d-nature," to use your terminology. There's no talk of any "c-nature" there, or anywhere else in Scripture as far as I can see.

STEPHANIE: Then how do you account for the fact that you are gay— sorry, same-sex attracted? You said earlier that you didn't choose to be that, and that you weren't abused or have a dysfunctional family life.

Dialogue 4

AMANDA: It is God's plan for me. God is sovereign and his ways are higher than mine. God's plan for all of us is to pursue holiness. He does not give us all the same challenges to achieve that. You and Dave have other challenges. Phil and I have this one. Phil is my friend and it breaks my heart to see him own his homosexuality and build a same-sex "marriage" on it.

DAVID: Then what is your opinion of the idea that your homosexual orientation is, or is the result of, a neurobiological condition in your body?

AMANDA: I'm skeptical about that, as I've said, but I'm not denying it, Dave. But whatever the neurobiology is, it doesn't excuse me from any responsibility to pursue God's goals for me. It strikes me, Steph, that the line you're taking is doing just that.

STEPHANIE: I'm really sorry you think that, Amanda. I was hoping you would understand that I was not trying to find a "soft" line to take on this subject. I believe in the pursuit of holiness as much as you do. I just disagree that same-sex attractions are in themselves sinful and as such constitute a challenge to one's pursuit of holiness.

DAVID: I agree with you on that point, Steph. The challenge comes with avoiding homosexual lust and behavior, not attraction per se. But so far you've put off saying one way or the other whether you believe that homosexual behavior in itself is sinful or not. So what's your view on that?

STEPHANIE: You're right, of course. I've said that it is not aligned with (human) nature, and that that nature is determined by God's design. But I've pushed back against Amanda's inference that it is sinful for just that reason. Amanda's inference is merely that—an inference. So now I am at a point of directly addressing the question of whether or not same-sex relationships, including same-sex marriage, are sinful. It's time for me to come clean on that. Here's the next card on the table.

Consider this diagram. Each of the four boxes A, B, C, and D names one of four categories of human sexual expression. The margin to the left names the moral or theological status of these forms of expression. I think we can all agree about the moral status of boxes A, C, and D. The question marks in box B indicate the possibility of disagreement about that. So far, we can conclude that Phil affirms the designation "Holy (not sinful)" for the B behavior, and Amanda and Dave deny that. Before I cast my vote, I need to explain my way toward it.

Moral Status	*Heterosexual Expression*	*Homosexual Expression*
Holy (*not sinful*)	**A** Sexual Union in Married, Exclusive, Covenanted, Unconditionally Committed Love	**B** Sexual Union in Married, Exclusive, Covenanted, Unconditionally Committed Love **????**
Unholy (*sinful*)	**C** Extramarital Lust Prostitution Non-consensual Sexual Assault Incest Adultery Pornography One-night stands, hook ups Seduction Exploitative (power play) Pedophilia Pederasty Sado-Masochism Ritualistic (temple rites) Etc. etc.	**D** Extramarital Lust Prostitution Non-consensual Sexual Assault Incest Adultery Pornography One-night stands, hook ups Seduction Exploitative (power play) Pedophilia Pederasty Sado-Masochism Ritualistic (temple rites) Etc. etc.

The first thing to say is that whenever the Bible condemns homosexuality, both the psychological states and the behavior, it condemns states and behaviors included in the D box, not necessarily that of the B box. So the Leviticus prohibition against "lying with a man as with a woman" is presumably against a single act, or a series of single acts, that are of a "hook up" nature and possibly one or more of the other behaviors in the D box. The behaviors of the male-bedders with the softies in 1 Corinthians and 1 Timothy would presumably come under lust, prostitution, perhaps adultery, possibly one-night stands, and pedophilia or pederasty. The orgies and other homosexual behaviors in ancient Rome and elsewhere probably have these in view as well, but also exploitation based on a power differential, given the power differences between the classes (aristocrats or free men generally as opposed to slaves). I want to make two points about this. First, the behaviors in the D box also occur in the C box, the only difference being that in the D box they are homosexual behaviors whereas in the C box they are heterosexual. The significance of this is that whether these behaviors occur in a homosexual or heterosexual context, they are all sinful sexual behaviors. So even if we transposed the forbidden behavior in the two Leviticus passages from a homosexual context to a heterosexual context, it would still be sinful and deserving of biblical condemnation. So also with the New Testament passages. Second, the only difference in biblical characterization between A/C and B/D, if my account so far has been correct, is that A/C behaviors are "natural" (even if the C behaviors are sinful) while the B/D behaviors are "unnatural." So, since the only difference between A and B is just that fact, it remains to be seen whether the B behavior is sinful. One thing we cannot say is that the B behavior is sinful *just because* the D behaviors are sinful. It's important to remember that the sinfulness of the D behaviors does not transfer automatically to the B behavior. (Recall Phil's complaint two weeks ago that many Christians "throw [his and James's relationship] into the same moral cesspool" as the perverted practices of the pagans referred to in Romans 1.) We cannot, therefore, conclude that the biblical condemnation of the D behaviors entails a condemnation of the B behavior.

So for me the crucial question turns out to be this:

> *Does God require gay people to comply with the heterosexual standard inherent in his design for human sexuality—their human d-nature—or does God accommodate his requirement to their actual God-created gay c-natures?*

AMANDA: Are you suggesting that God might have a *different* standard for same-sex attracted people than for straight people when it comes to forming relationships that include sexual activity? Where in the Bible do you find anything remotely like that?

STEPHANIE: I'm saying that that is a possibility we should seriously consider, Amanda. And you're right, I don't find any such suggestion anywhere in the Bible. But then—

AMANDA: How can you do that, Steph? If you really hold the Bible to be authoritative, shouldn't you stick to what the Bible says and not go beyond it?

STEPHANIE: What I was going to say is that I also don't find in the Bible anything that shows God holding those he created with a particular impairment to *the same* standard as those he created without that impairment.

DAVID: Sorry, Steph. That sounds like an argument from silence to me. The best that can be said is that what you're suggesting *might* be the case, but we should be careful in just assuming that it *is* the case without some actual evidence.

STEPHANIE: I'm not suggesting that I *know* it to be the case, Dave. But it is worth investigating whether or not it might be the case. And in doing so we should be aware that we are all—you two as well as I—coloring outside the biblical lines. There are no texts in the Bible to which either side can appeal to settle this question.

AMANDA: How are Dave and I "coloring outside the biblical lines" if we hold that the Bible gives no basis for assuming that God would give an exemption to same-sex-attracted people from his revealed standards for sex and marriage?

STEPHANIE: You're right, Amanda. The Bible does not give any basis for assuming that. Since, I admit, the Bible gives no explicit acknowledgement of any gap between our sexual d-natures and c-natures, and shows no awareness of an unchosen neurobiological origin of homosexuality, it follows that the Bible gives no explicit reason for thinking that God gives any such exemption. But what if the biblical authors, Paul in particular, had known what we now know about such an unchosen, inborn condition? As I said last week, the "construct" regarding homosexuality that Paul is operating with is different from ours. But what if Paul had had *our* construct of homosexuality available to him? Would he still have described homosexuality as involving a voluntary *exchange* from a universal inborn heterosexual condition to an acquired homosexual one? And even if Paul should reject our contemporary construct, are we twenty-first-century believers obligated to deny what we now know to be true? Isn't that itself a "suppression" of a truth God has revealed, though not in the Bible? Does being "biblical" require such a narrow interpretation? Could being "biblical" include an affirmation of *all* truth, wherever it is to be found—both within the Bible and outside of it? Isn't *all truth* linked to Jesus who is *the* Truth?

DAVID: It looks like either way we're taking a chance in claiming to discern the mind of God. Perhaps Amanda is playing it safe: her principle is that if God's permission is not explicitly stated in the Bible, we should take God to be forbidding it. You on the other hand, Steph, are sticking your neck out. Your principle is that we might well be entitled to take God to be permitting it in light of our more complete, even if not totally complete, knowledge of homosexuality.

AMANDA: I'd rather be safe than sorry.

DAVID: But that means that you think it's better to forbid something that God permits—if Phil is right, and perhaps Stephanie also—than to permit something that God forbids—if you are right. I'm not sure that this is necessarily the case. The Pharisees were notorious for forbidding things that God permitted (like healing on the Sabbath, consorting with "sinners," and so forth). Jesus reserved his sternest rebukes for them. Even the disciples provoked Jesus's censure when they forbade mothers from bringing their little children to Jesus.

PHILIP: As I read the Bible, the heart of God is always for inclusion. And even if we were to include those whom God might not include, we should just leave it to God to do the excluding. We don't need to weed out the tares from the wheat before harvest time. That's God's job, and he will do it in his own time and his own way.

STEPHANIE: That's a great reminder, Phil.

AMANDA: I'm sorry, guys, I can't go there with you. The Bible's condemnation of homosexuality is unconditional, not conditioned upon what we readers of the Bible might happen to know or not know at any particular time in history. Steph, I hear you saying that if Paul had been better informed about homosexuality, if his knowledge had been more "complete" (your word), he would not have condemned it the way he did in Romans 1. Wasn't Paul inspired by the Holy Spirit when he wrote those words? And if so, isn't that authoritative Scripture for us, neither to be added to nor taken away from? Aren't you in fact disagreeing with the Bible? What are you really saying about the word of God?

STEPHANIE: I'm saying that the biblical authors were people of their own time, not our time. The Bible is no doubt God's word. But that Word comes to us by way of human authors who were situated in certain places and times in history that are different from ours. These authors spoke the word of God to people who, like them, were situated in those particular places at those particular times. These people were the *primary* audiences to whom God's word was directly spoken. We in the twenty-first century, on the other hand, are the *secondary* audience. And we inhabit a very different culture from those of the primary audiences. We are for the most part aware of a "cultural distance" between those ancient cultures and our own. For example, slavery as a social institution was an accepted social "fact" in the ancient world. None of the biblical authors protest against slavery as such. Biblical authors decry the abuses of slavery and seek to mitigate its evils, and Paul proclaims that unity in Christ transcends the master-slave relationship (Galatians 3:28). But neither Paul nor any other biblical author condemns slavery as intrinsically evil or advocates for its abolition. Much the same could be said for patriarchy.

AMANDA: This appeal to "cultural distance" can be very slippery, Stephanie, as I'm sure you're aware. Some writers invoke it as a blank check to justify rejection of any transcendent, supernatural reality, on the ground that belief in such a reality is out of step with modern culture. They "demythologize" the Bible so as to render it acceptable to the "modern" mind. It is hard to see such moves as consistent with any commitment to the authority of the Bible.

STEPHANIE: You're absolutely right, Amanda. The belief in a transcendent, supernatural, personal source of the material world who acts within that world and reveals himself to humankind is foundational to any biblical worldview. What I meant, rather, is that the Bible sometimes tolerates, even if it does not endorse, cultural beliefs and practices that the Bible's own core principles and values eventually undermine. The Bible seems to tolerate practices like polygamy and, as I just said, even slavery, a practice based on the belief that it is okay for some human beings to own, buy, or sell other human beings as pieces of property. Parts of the Bible seem to endorse patriarchy, which is based on the belief that women are of lesser value than men. The idea that all human beings have equal dignity and worth, regardless of race, gender or social status, is at its core an insight that comes from the Bible itself.

DAVID: So where are you going with this as far as homosexuality is concerned?

STEPHANIE: Just as we have accepted a cultural distance between the time of the biblical authors and our own, so I think we should accept what earlier I called a "cognitive distance" between what the biblical authors knew in their time and what we know in our own. The biblical authors did not know and could not have known most of what we now know about the natural world through science. They knew nothing about modern astronomy. Their beliefs—for example, the belief that the earth is fixed at the center of the observable universe and that the sun, moon, planets, and stars revolve around the earth—have been overturned in succeeding centuries. Their ancient beliefs make them neither deceivers nor ignorant fools, despite the fact that those beliefs can no longer be maintained in light of what we know now. And so it has turned out that the beliefs of the biblical authors—Paul's in particular—about the origin and nature of homosexuality have also been superseded. To put this in the language of "disagreeing with the Bible" is way too crass, Amanda. That kind of language is spoiling for a fight. A better way to think of it is this: God, through the medium of scientific research and the stories that modern gay people tell about their lives, has now revealed what was not revealed to the biblical writers, including Paul. So, taking God's entire revelation into account, not just the Bible, I have concluded that the "crucial question" I just posed is not only appropriate, but actually inevitable. And to answer this question we cannot appeal to any series of biblical texts; we need to look at this as a broader ethical issue: *Given what we know about God from Scripture, how would God expect us to treat those among us who suffer from impairments of various sorts—including this impairment in particular?*

DAVID: Okay, I see where you're going with this. Not that I agree with your approach, but I'd like to hear how you'll develop it in fashioning a defense of same-sex marriage—if I'm right in suspecting that that's where you're going.

STEPHANIE: Well, continue with me in my exploration. First, something about the term, "same-sex marriage." People ask—in fact I ask: Is same-sex "marriage" really *marriage*? From the divine design perspective (based on our d-nature) the answer is no: heterosexuality and therefore only heterosexual marriage is in accordance with God's design. But from the accommodationist perspective, based on how God actually creates some people gay (their c-nature), it opens the *possibility* for a covenanted union between two same-sex partners, based upon the taking and living out of vows of mutual faithfulness and support, to count as a marriage. So, is a same-sex marriage really a marriage? My answer is no and yes. To be sure, a same-sex marriage falls short of God's design for marriage. But it does not follow that it cannot count as a marriage in any sense at all. A central aspect of God's design for marriage—lifelong, exclusive, and faithful companionship and commitment to one other person is reflected in it, even if another central aspect—sexual difference—is not. Whether you choose to think of a same-sex "marriage" as a real *marriage* or not is to my mind a matter of personal conviction or preference. The choice of terminology seems to me to be of no ethical consequence. What *is* of ethical consequence is the question of whether we have good reason to think that God not only permits but *actually blesses* such relationships, as Phil and James have concluded, or whether God withholds his permission and blessing, as Amanda and probably you as well, Dave, appear to believe. So we'll need to take into account not only the Bible's homosexuality and marriage texts, but also the broad ethical principles we find in the Bible, as well as everything we know about homosexuality today.

DAVID: Well, Steph, I have to tell you that there is nothing in the Bible that encourages me to think that God would permit or bless these relationships. Its verdict on homosexual activity is uniformly negative. And I see nothing on the ethical horizon that would allow for exceptions. I have to be honest with you: I'm skeptical about your "accommodationist perspective."

STEPHANIE: Thanks for your candor, David. Let me continue on my present path though, and do continue to express any reservations you have as we go along.

AMANDA: So how do you see the biblical texts on marriage, Jesus's teaching in Matthew 19 and the Ephesians 5 passage? Do you side with Phil's account of it, or do you accept Dave's critique of Phil's account?

STEPHANIE: On the question of what these passages actually teach, I agree with David. However, these passages all reflect the divine design perspective. They do not consider or make room for the accommodationist perspective at all because of the Bible's assumption I've already noted: the Bible shows no awareness of what I have called the "gap" between what God has designed and what God actually creates, at least in the area of human gender and sexuality. According to the teaching of these passages—and I would also include Genesis 2 where the concepts of the "*ezer kenegdo*" and the "one flesh union" come up—marriage is definitely a husband-wife relationship, not a husband-husband or wife-wife relationship. But as I've said, our present knowledge of homosexuality today begs for a consideration of the accommodationist perspective.

AMANDA: I'm very concerned about how you treat the word of God, Steph. You seem to consider it merely a record of Jewish and early Christian opinions written down over centuries of time, many of which are now outdated and should be cast aside. You've created a gap that is more fundamental and more consequential than your gap between our "d-nature" and our various "c-natures," and that is the gap between what the Bible says and what you say we moderns should believe about a given subject such as homosexuality. I'm sorry, but I can't go there with you. If the Bible is not inerrant, and *we* are the judges of what's true and false in the Bible, why believe anything that's in the Bible? Why not just go with whatever we in our own wisdom decide whatever is acceptable to believe? Your approach places the infallible Bible under the authority of fallible human reason, rather than placing fallible human reason under the authority of an infallible Bible.

STEPHANIE: Thanks for your honesty and directness, Amanda. I don't agree with your characterization of my approach, though. I reject the characterization of my view of Scripture as "merely a record of Jewish and early

Christian opinions." All of Scripture is divinely inspired and authoritative. But Scripture must be interpreted and applied correctly. Its application to us today may or may not be the same as its application to the primary audience.

DAVID: We're again at that point where the two of you have different starting points in regard to the authority of Scripture. Here's another way of putting that difference. You both agree that God inspired the Bible and used human authors to write it. So the Bible is the word of God mediated through the words of human beings. This duality recalls the theory of the "Two Natures of Christ": Christ is both fully human and fully divine. But you disagree about the implications of this duality in the case of the Bible. Descriptors like "inerrant" and "infallible" emphasize divine authorship: since God inspired the Bible and God cannot lie, the Bible's statements cannot be false. By contrast, concepts like "cultural distance" and "cognitive distance" lay stress on human authorship: the practices, institutions, and assumptions about the world that characterize the historical situations of the human authors and contextualize what they write are not necessarily normative for us to believe in or to practice today. A fully satisfactory "doctrine of Scripture" must hold both of these two aspects of the Bible in balance. We will not always agree on how that balance should be struck, as seems to be the case with the two of you right now.

STEPHANIE: Thanks, Dave. That's helpful. Amanda and I should probably take a time-out from our discussion of homosexuality to dig more deeply into those foundational issues. Unfortunately that would take us too far afield. For now, though, we'll just have to agree to disagree.

DAVID: So let me ask you straight out, Steph. In terms of the "crucial question" you posed just now, do you yourself believe in the accommodationist perspective? That God accommodates his standards for sex and marriage to gay and lesbian people? That they are not required to comply with the heterosexual standard inherent in God's design for human sexuality? And that God blesses faithful, monogamous same-sex relationships just as he blesses heterosexual marriage?

STEPHANIE: So now I'll put my last card on the table. The answer I give is yes, Dave, I do believe that. I believe that, based upon what I know about the character of God as he is revealed in the Bible and the broad ethical principles taught there, God would indeed permit people who are gay to form same-sex relationships, including what I personally would be quite prepared to call "marriage." If I am wrong, if I have misunderstood the Bible, I would be grateful to have that shown to me. I've laid out how I understand and apply the biblical texts that speak to this issue, and I have not been persuaded that those who disagree with my answer have a better understanding or application of those texts. I have prayed about this for a very long time and have evaluated people's arguments on all sides of this question in much the same way as we've been doing ourselves for the last four weeks.

DAVID: Can you explain the reasons for the position you've taken?

STEPHANIE: Yes. There are several. Negatively, as I've explained, I reject Amanda's inference from the premise "not conforming to God's design"— with which I agree—to the conclusion "therefore sinful"—with which I disagree. I do not confuse the behaviors of the D box, which I agree truly are sinful, with the behavior of the B box, just as I would not confuse the behaviors in the C box with that in the A box. At the risk of over-repetition, I see the Bible as condemning D behaviors as sin, but being silent about the B behavior.

AMANDA: I don't know what to tell you, Steph. We are just poles apart on that.

STEPHANIE: Maybe so, Amanda. We may just have to let that go. My first positive ethical argument is an argument from analogy. Let's consider the question of what our obligations are to people who live with an impairment that most other people do not live with. In every other case the answer is clear: as I've already suggested, our obligation is to provide available resources and support to enable them to live lives as close to normal—that is, without the impairment—as possible. My eyeglasses and Dave's asthma medications are examples of this. No one tells me that because I cannot see clearly I must resign myself to going through life with near blindness. No one tells Dave that he just has to live with his asthma untreated. By the same token, no one has a right to tell someone who is not sexually attracted to the opposite sex to go through life without the sexual fulfillment that marriage is meant for.

PHILIP: I agree with you, Steph.

STEPHANIE: My second positive ethical argument builds on the first. It concerns the idea of "human flourishing." This idea is gaining traction in contemporary Christian ethical reflection. The idea is not of Christian origin—indeed it derives from Aristotle (4th century BCE). Aristotle believed that we humans "flourish" to the extent that the capacities or abilities that define us as human are given the opportunity to be fulfilled or realized. Christians can and do adapt this idea in the following way: God uniquely creates each human person with a set of capacities or abilities some of which are shared by all people, others of which are common only to a subset of people, and still others which may be unique to a particular individual. Each of us is a created "package" of capacities. God's goal for each one of us, then, is the maximum realization of whatever capacities are in our set—capacities created by him—all within the context of our call to love God above all and our neighbors as ourselves, and to deploy the "fruit of the Spirit" (Galatians 5:22). That's what human flourishing looks like. We owe it to our neighbors to help them achieve that, by allowing the development and exercise of all, not just some, of their God-given capacities.

DAVID: Aristotle was a genius! There's so much in his thought that is illuminating for a Christian worldview!

PHILIP: I thought you were a fan of Plato, Dave.

DAVID: Of both, Phil. Of each in his own way.

STEPHANIE: Anyhow, the implications of this for our question are as follows: In general, gay as well as straight people have within their "package" the capacity to fall in love and develop deep romantic relationships, and the aspiration, even the longing, to intimately share their lives with one other person, be exclusively devoted to that person throughout their lives and express that devotion in acts of sexual intimacy. This is one of their created capacities they share with straight people. However, unlike their straight counterparts and through no fault of their own, they lack the capacity to enter into that experience with someone of the opposite sex. In believing that God requires them to deny or suppress a capacity they have (that of forming an intimate exclusive relationship with one other person) because of a capacity that they lack (that of forming such a relationship with someone of the opposite sex), many if not most Christians deny gays and lesbians the opportunity, even the right, to exercise one of their God-given capacities. To that extent these Christians impede instead of promote the flourishing of their gay neighbors. It is typical of such Christians to believe that entering into an intimate relationship with someone of their own sex is contrary to human flourishing. Their reason for saying this is their a priori, biblically anchored belief—with which I totally agree—that you cannot possibly live a flourishing life if you live outside the boundaries of God's will. Couple this with their belief—with which I don't agree—that living within an exclusive and enduring romantic homosexual relationship is living outside those boundaries, and their conclusion follows. But if, as I've argued, it is far from clear whether God's will for gay people requires them to live up to the standard of his design (their d-nature) or is accommodated to their individual gay c-natures, it is not clear that this a priori criterion for their flourishing should apply.

PHILIP: Nicely put, Steph. It sounds like these Christians you're talking about disagree with God about how he made Amanda and me.

AMANDA: Please speak for yourself, Phil.

STEPHANIE: Anyhow, we should remember that human flourishing is also an empirical matter. We can very often just see with our own eyes whether an animal, a plant, or a human individual is thriving (which is the same thing as flourishing) or not. And so it will be obvious that living a lifetime with deep unfulfilled desires is to that extent failing to thrive. In reading some of the biographies of gay Christians who choose celibacy but admit to a crushing loneliness, I often sense just such a failure to thrive.

AMANDA: Wait a minute, Steph. Are you saying that sexual fulfillment as such is necessary to human flourishing? That one can't flourish unless one is sexually fulfilled?

STEPHANIE: I said "to that extent," Amanda. We don't have to have all of our desires fulfilled in order to thrive. Very few of us have all our desires fulfilled. Some people get on very well despite struggling with unfulfilled sexual desires. For others this is a greater burden.

PHILIP: Knowing myself, I can honestly say that living without the hope of sexual fulfillment that marriage is meant for would count seriously against my prospects of thriving. I have not been granted the gift of celibacy. Moreover, to struggle against my same-sex attractions, as many Christians insist I must do—and as Amanda feels she must do—instead of accepting the way God has created me is very much a recipe for failing to thrive.

AMANDA: There are few things that are as dangerous as false self-acceptance, Phil. Your and Stephanie's claim that God created you and me "gay" is a snare and a delusion! It makes me sad, really sad, for you—for both of you.

STEPHANIE: We knew at the outset that these conversations would be difficult. But let me move on to my third argument, which builds on the other two. By prohibiting gay people from participating in monogamous relationships that involve sexual expression, we impose an intolerable burden on many if not most of them. True, sex isn't everything in a marriage, but it is pretty central, and it is unfair to gay people to minimize its importance. True, many people have wonderful lives without sex. But to remind gay people of that is the height of insensitivity, especially to those like Phil who are neither called to nor gifted for celibacy. Many gay Christians are navigating their sexual lives successfully without sexual expression, perhaps by forming deep "spiritual friendships" of the sort that Dave described last week, with other gay and possibly some straight friends. That is indeed a blessing to be celebrated. But we should not forget that this is a voluntary choice on their part, even if a conscience-driven one. It is cruel on the part of the wider conservative Christian community to hold such gay Christians up as "poster children," as models for how *all* Christian gay people ought to navigate their sexual lives. To hold such Christians up as following the "biblical" path (implying that gay Christians who do not choose that path aren't making a biblical choice) weaponizes that term against gay brothers and sisters like Phil who, based on *their* study of the Bible, have felt free to make a different choice.

PHILIP: I've noticed a tendency within many Christian communities to use the term "biblical" to baptize their own theological positions, and "unbiblical" to excommunicate those with which they disagree. That's a conversation stopper if ever there was one. Once Christians declare a position to be "unbiblical," they give themselves permission to condemn it and to warn other believers against it.

STEPHANIE: The antidote to that is to remember—again—that while God's word is infallible, our interpretations of it are not, so a degree of humility and charity is called for on all sides.

AMANDA: Wait a minute, Steph. Are you saying that as long as there is a covenantal relationship, sexual expression is okay for a gay couple? This sounds a lot like saying that as long as that expression is consensual, it's not wrong. But in the case of straight people, we as Christians wouldn't want to say anything like this, nor would the Bible permit it. I think we all agree on that. Sexual expression is permitted only after, first, the couple is legally married and in possession of a marriage certificate, and second, the couple has made a vow of mutual faithfulness "before God and these witnesses." How does that apply to gay couples?

PHILIP: I think I can answer that, Amanda. James and I have been investigating a number of churches as a possible venue for our wedding ceremony. Several insist that they will not host the ceremony or have their pastors officiate unless we have a state-issued marriage certificate in hand. This is a requirement that both James and I are totally on board with. Now that same-sex marriage is legally permitted in every state, this will not present a problem. And of course our vows will also be said "in front of God and these witnesses" during the ceremony.

STEPHANIE: One could argue that the legalization of same-sex marriage, instead of being a threat to the church, as so many Christians believe it to be, is instead a gift to the church. It makes same-sex marriage as legally binding as heterosexual marriage. So the traditional principle of "no sex before or outside of a legally binding, publicly declared covenanted marriage relationship" is not undermined or qualified, however one decides the question of whether same-sex marriage is truly marriage. Consensuality is far from sufficient for engaging in a sexual relationship, regardless of the sexual orientation of the parties involved. And, as to my point about "flourishing," neither straight nor gay couples will flourish sexually outside of these boundaries.

PHILIP: Thanks for clarifying this, Stephanie. This is well worth emphasizing, in view of a popular perception that same-sex marriage is in some way looser than traditional heterosexual marriage.

STEPHANIE: My fourth argument, related to all three of the previous ones, is that by refusing to honor same-sex monogamous relationships, refusing to celebrate and support the vows same-sex couples make to each other and to include them fully in their churches and other communities, conservative Christians are both alienating them and losing them. People will go where they are accepted. Multitudes of young gay men and women who have grown up in a church have, like Phil, been rejected by their churches—many by their own Christian families—and unlike Phil, they have drifted away, often toward secular gay communities that accept them but that are morally and spiritually destructive. Their lives have been turned into spiritual wastelands. This ought to be deeply troubling to communities that name the name of Jesus. Often in Christian communities gay people are beckoned in with one arm and stiff-armed out with the other. Churches that style themselves as "welcoming but not affirming" are not attracting gay believers in any great numbers. Often these churches are afraid to look hard at both the Bible, as we have done, and at reality. That's not Jesus's way.

DAVID: I tend to agree on that point, Steph. But about your cumulative argument that we should approve of same-sex relationships—or at least not disapprove of them—there's something deep within me that holds me back from seeing things your way. Whether homosexual acts even in the context of a faithful monogamous relationship are sin or not, there's a deep sense in my gut that rebels against the very idea. I can't get rid of it. It seems just wrong!

AMANDA: That's the Holy Spirit, David! Don't quench his voice!

STEPHANIE: I would call it the voice of conscience, Dave. Your conscience about this question has been formed by years of teaching you've received and reading you've done that an affirming position is in conflict with the Bible. The Bible calls us to respect and not bind one another's consciences (Romans 14). This is an essential element of our Christian freedom. But conscience is not an infallible guide. It is not always the voice of the Holy Spirit. Remember that Huckleberry Finn thought he was acting *against* his conscience when he helped his friend Jim escape from slavery to freedom. His conscience that it was wrong to help a slave escape was formed by the pro-slavery society in which he was raised. Sometimes our consciences need to be brought into alignment with how God is actually speaking. This is something that all Christians should individually consider; it cannot be legislated.

PHILIP: When I was struggling with my gay feelings back in high school, I sensed exactly what you're sensing, Dave. "This is just wrong! How can I be like this? God, do you still love me? You obviously didn't create me this way! What did I do to get this way?" It wasn't until I came to sense God's overwhelming love for me and his purpose for my life as a gay person that I found peace. I've given over my entire life, including my sexuality, to God to use as he wills. He accepts me exactly as I am, not as something I am not and cannot hope to be.

DAVID: Well, maybe so, Phil. But may I be brutally honest? I find that imagining two people of the same sex doing sexual things together pretty disgusting, if I may say so, and I think most straight people would feel the same way.

PHILIP: Thanks for your brutal honesty, Dave. Thanks for owning up to the most sensitive aspect of our entire discussion. This is what some people call the "ick factor" as it relates to people's feelings about homosexuality. It is at the root of the self-loathing that many gay people, especially gay men, feel about themselves—a feeling some never get over. In my more cynical moments I find myself wondering whether it is disgust, and not so much theology, that motivates opposition to same-sex marriage. What do you think, Dave? Could this be true in your own case? Could it be that the disgust that we all properly feel at the depraved practices of Paul's world (and often of our own) spills over into a gut-level disapproval of gay men or women who want to marry each other, like James and myself? I'll make this personal: how do you see *me*, David?

DAVID: I'm struggling, Phil. You're a great friend, and I've benefited from our friendship enormously over the few years we've known each other. I can't ever put that aside. At the same time—

PHILIP: You don't have to say it, Dave. I just want you to know that I understand. I will pray for you. But even as I pray, I want to challenge you to come and see gay folks, both men and women, as Jesus sees us, or Paul, when he says in 2 Corinthians 5:16 that he no longer sees anyone "according to the flesh," with worldly vision. I pray that your eyes may be opened to seeing me, and all gay people, with spiritual vision, as Paul came to see Jesus after his conversion.

DAVID: Thanks, Phil. I'm sensing a need, deep within my spirit, for that kind of conversion in myself. Thanks for praying for me. I'm not sure how this will affect my position on same-sex marriage, but I do need a new way of seeing.

STEPHANIE: And this new way of seeing is really the more important thing, Dave. *(After a pause)* This is a holy moment, and I don't want to break the spell. All I would add, Dave, is that like conscience, disgust is never a reliable guide to discerning what's right or wrong. Not very long ago many white conservative Christians were repelled by the very idea of interracial marriage. The mental image of a white bride escorted by a white father down the aisle to be given in marriage to a black groom (or vice versa) was abhorrent to them. In fact, right up until the middle of the last century many such Christians tried to argue from the Bible that interracial marriages were contrary to God's will. Only during the second half of that century were their arguments shown to be what they really are: theologically indefensible and a cover for racism.

AMANDA: Steph, you and Phil aren't suggesting that opposition to same-sex marriage is on a par with opposition to interracial marriage, are you? Or that the historic, biblical case for exclusive heterosexual marriage is theologically indefensible and merely a cover for homophobia?

STEPHANIE: We're not suggesting any such thing, Amanda. We're only suggesting that subjective factors like feelings and conscience are not reliable guides to forming a responsible, spiritually mature and well-informed position on a moral issue. They are not substitutes for the kind of careful study of the Bible and informed theological and ethical deliberation we ourselves have engaged in over these last weeks.

DAVID: Steph, do you want to say more in defense of the position you've taken, or are we done?

PHILIP: Stephanie, before you finish, let me remind you that a while ago you mentioned something about what you knew from the Bible about the character of God—that you believe that God would permit people who are gay to form same-sex relationships. That's really huge. You can't just leave that hanging; you need to say more about that.

STEPHANIE: You're right, Phil. Thanks for not letting that slip by. So this is the question I ask myself: Is the God of the Bible, who is supremely revealed in Jesus, the sort of God who requires all people at all times to submit to the rules or laws that he himself has instituted, or does God sometimes bend his own rules, allowing exceptions to accommodate human needs? I find the best answer in the New Testament, in Jesus's attitude toward keeping the Sabbath. Jesus's acts of healing on the Sabbath and his disciples' act of harvesting grain on the Sabbath to satisfy their hunger were denounced by the Pharisees as violations of the law requiring abstention from work on the Sabbath. In his response Jesus cites the example of David and his cohorts being offered the consecrated bread in the tabernacle to eat—a violation of a divine command. You can read about this in Matthew 12 or Mark 2. Jesus famously sums up his response by saying that the Sabbath was made for people, not people for the Sabbath, and that he himself is Lord of the Sabbath. By this declaration Jesus did not abrogate the Sabbath law, but insisted that this and by implication God's other laws were instituted to serve people, rather than people to serve the law. Serving the needs of people has priority over keeping the law. Being unaccommodating to the needs of people is a greater sin than breaking a particular law.

DAVID: So are you saying that same-sex "marriage," though not conforming to God's design, is something that God permits in the same way that God permits works of healing and satisfying hunger on the Sabbath?

AMANDA: And are you saying that marriage is "a human need" like being healed from a disease? That's a huge stretch, Steph!

STEPHANIE: I am trying to discern the heart of God on the subject of same-sex "married" relationships, acknowledging that God's design for human sexuality is heterosexuality and that God's design for marriage is heterosexual marriage. Would God bend his own standards to accommodate those people who for some reason he did not create to have a heterosexual orientation so that they, too, could have their need—yes, need, Amanda—for an enduring, intimate relationship with one other person actually met? The New Testament passages about Jesus's attitude to the Sabbath do not definitively prove anything one way or the other about this issue, but they do encourage me to believe that God's heart is for accommodation. You are certainly free to disagree, but if you do, the burden of proof is yours, not mine.

So, now I'm done with presenting my case. And I think our four-week stretch of conversations is at an end. I think it's clear to all four of us that we did not achieve the consensus we had hoped for. At crucial points we have not been able to persuade one another. Now we have a choice to make. One option is for each of us to become entrenched in her or his own position and contend for it by way of writing of books, articles, book reviews, blogs, and the like against each of the others, each of us claiming that *"I"* have the true biblical perspective and that *"you"* don't. This will not lessen the turmoil in the conservative Christian communities we're part of. This route is never-ending; we each will always think we have a better argument, a clearer view of the Bible, and probably a keener sense that *"my"* way of seeing the issue is God's way. The other option is to learn to obey the Bible. In Ephesians 4:3 Paul tells us to be "eager to maintain the unity of the Spirit in the bond of peace." I think it's fair to say that on this issue we've all but forgotten that command.

DAVID: I'm sorry to interrupt, Steph. We've already gone far past our usual time and perhaps should call it a night. Do you all think that we could schedule one more conversation? The challenge implied by your last comment is too important to ignore. What do the rest of you think?

AMANDA: I don't think I can make it next Friday night. We're well into November and I'm beginning to feel the pressure as the semester winds down, especially with the Thanksgiving recess coming up and due dates for assignments fast approaching. Still, I definitely feel the importance, not to say urgency, of responding to God's imperative to maintain our unity in the Spirit, despite our lack of agreement on the issues we've talked about.

PHILIP: I agree. It's so easy, and so "human," for those on one side of these issues to simply dismiss or break fellowship those on the other side. Let's look at our individual calendars and see if we can come up with a time we can all set aside for this. It needn't be a Friday night. I don't think it should take us more than an hour or so.

STEPHANIE: That shouldn't be a problem. Let's take a look . . .

The four take out their calendars and agree on a time acceptable to all.

Questions for Reflection
and Discussion on Dialogue 4

1. Can you relate to any aspect of Stephanie's story? Is there someone you are close to who is gay? If so, how does their sexuality affect your relationship?

2. Stephanie reframes the discussion in terms of the seven parameters she lays out. Amanda takes exception to Stephanie's approach. Why? With whom are you inclined to agree?

3. How does Stephanie's view of a "creation order" for human gender and sexuality differ from both Amanda's and Philip's? Do you believe that there is such a creation order? Explain.

4. Stephanie characterizes same-sex desire as a "malfunction," leading to what she calls an "impairment." What does she mean by this? Philip disagrees. What do you think?

5. Is experiencing same-sex desires a case of "sin baked in"? Discuss with reference to the disagreement between Amanda and Stephanie.

6. How do the four characters disagree with one another on the question of whether God does or does not create people gay? Why is this an important issue? With which of the characters do you find yourself mostly in agreement? Explain your own answer to this question.

7. Explain in your own words Stephanie's distinction between a person's "design nature" and their "created nature," and her claim that the latter does not always conform to the former. How does she account for the "gap"? Do you find this distinction helpful in accounting for homosexuality? Discuss.

8. What, for Stephanie, is the "crucial question" in the debate about whether God allows space for faithful, monogamous same-sex relationships? Do you agree that her way of framing that question is an appropriate way to frame it?

9. Stephanie supports her own answer to her crucial question by a number of arguments. Summarize and evaluate her arguments.

10. Have you encountered expressions of the "ick factor" in listening to other people (or in your own thinking)? How would you respond?

11. How do you yourself read "God's heart" in relation to the permissibility of same-sex marriage? Explain.

12. How do you "see" people who are gay? Do you think you might need a "conversion" the way David came to believe he does?

Dialogue 4½

A week or so later.

DAVID: Thanks, everyone, for making time for this extra meeting. To start us off, Stephanie, do you want to recapitulate the challenge you left us with at our last meeting?

STEPHANIE: Certainly. I said that, having failed to persuade one another, we have a choice to make: either to remain entrenched in our own various positions and do battle with one another, or find a way to maintain the "unity of the Spirit" that Paul calls us to in Ephesians. The former might be our natural default and tempting, but it is not an option Scripture gives us. The latter is what we're called to pursue. But we need the Holy Spirit to illumine the path.

AMANDA: So what does that look like? I have to confess that on an issue on which we are so far apart that could be a real challenge.

STEPHANIE: It would mean that we *intentionally create space* for one another. In other words, on this issue, that we actively embrace pluralism— the idea that we are a better, stronger, more Christ-like community if we include rather than exclude others who embrace points of view with which we may disagree, even strongly, and leave it to God to sort out those disagreements. After all, what we have in Christ is so much stronger, so much deeper, so much more abundant, than these issues that divide us.

AMANDA: So let's imagine that we all belong to the same local church. Would our commitment to unity include permitting same-sex "marriage" ceremonies in our church, even when some within the church like myself would have strong, principled, Bible-based objections to such ceremonies?

STEPHANIE: Well, what do *you* think, Amanda? Let's make this personal. What would you think Christ would have *you* do? Would he have you join a church in which, first, such weddings were permitted and same-sex married couples were part of the community and not restricted in any way and, second, one that fully respected, protected and supported your conscientious objections against such weddings and such relationships?

AMANDA: It's hard to imagine such a church. And even if there were one, I don't know if I would be up for that challenge.

DAVID: The challenge goes both ways. Most churches that are "welcoming and affirming" pride themselves on being "progressive" and sneer at churches and individuals who object to same-sex marriages. It would be a challenge to such a church to "fully respect, protect, and support" those with conscientious objections.

PHILIP: What would guidance in our imaginary church look like? I mean, suppose that James and I had been part this church before we got engaged, and during the "time out" period I mentioned we sought counsel from its spiritual leaders on whether or not to go ahead with our marriage. How might these leaders respond?

STEPHANIE: It should be their role not to nudge you one way or the other, but to help you discern how God may be calling you. How is God speaking to you, through the Bible but also through the circumstances of your life? How do you see God's call on your life best fulfilled? Which choice would help you to serve Christ better? And, of course, what is your conscience saying to you?

AMANDA: I thought you said last time that conscience is not a reliable guide in ethical decision-making.

STEPHANIE: I did, Amanda. It is not final. It is not definitive. You and Phil have different consciences about same-sex marriage, and you can't both be right. But the Bible teaches that if you act *against* your conscience, your action becomes sin *to you*, even if the act is not in itself wrong. The church has a responsibility to safeguard the consciences of its members. So the same church leaders who would permit Phil to go forward with his marriage to James should also discourage you, Amanda, possibly even warn you against forming a relationship with another woman as long as your conscience considers it sin.

DAVID: That's a tall order for any church. Are there any biblical passages that provide guidance?

STEPHANIE: In our conversations we've referenced Romans 14 a couple of times. It's now time to allow it to impact our thinking more fully. Here's an extract of some relevant verses from that chapter:

> Welcome [one another], but do not quarrel over opinions. One person believes he may eat anything, while [another] eats only vegetables. Let not the one who eats despise the one who abstains, and let not the one who abstains pass judgment on the one who eats, for God has welcomed him. Who are you to pass judgment on the servant of another? It is before his own master that he stands or falls. And he will be upheld, for the Lord is able to make him stand.
>
> One person esteems one day as better than another, while another esteems all days alike. Each one should be fully convinced in his own mind. The one who observes the day, observes it in honor of the Lord. The one who eats, eats in honor of the Lord, since he gives thanks to God, while the one who abstains, abstains in honor of the Lord and gives thanks to God.
>
> Why do you pass judgment on your brother? Or you, why do you despise your brother? For we will all stand before the judgment seat of God. So then each of us will give an account of himself to God. Therefore let us not pass judgment on one another any longer, but rather decide never to put a stumbling block or hindrance in the way of a brother. By what you eat, do not destroy the one for whom Christ died. So then let us pursue what makes for peace and for mutual upbuilding. The faith that you have, keep between yourself and God.

Remember the context. Although the eating of meat as such is not mentioned in this passage (the contrast is between omnivores and vegetarians), the young church at Rome, made up, as we've seen, of both Jewish and gentile converts, was divided between those who had no qualms about eating meat from animals that had been sacrificed to pagan idols and those who believed that eating such meat was serious sin. Rather than adjudicating the "meat eating issue" by just preaching what he does in 1 Corinthians 8:4–6—perhaps telling the vegetarians to just "get over it"—Paul calls them to what we might describe as "unity through forbearance." Accept one another and do not judge one another. Give space to someone else who does not share your conscience about a disputable matter. Do not impose your own conscience on anyone else who, like yourself, is ultimately accountable only to God. Do not judge but leave that job to God.

AMANDA: Are you suggesting that those who, like me, object to same-sex marriage should tolerate sin? Isn't there a huge difference between vegetarians tolerating omnivores and people who share my position on homosexuality tolerating same-sex relationships if we believe that those relationships are seriously sinful?

STEPHANIE: The vegetarians in the church would have thought that eating meat sacrificed to idols was just as "seriously sinful" as you believe same-sex relationships are. It will not seem very sinful to us—in fact Paul is pretty clear in 1 Corinthians 8 that it is not—but that's a matter of historical perspective. Who knows, perhaps a future generation of Christians will think that same-sex marriages are not "seriously sinful" at all and will look back on our day from their perspective and wonder what the fuss was all about. In any case, whatever the matter in dispute, Paul's exhortation to exercise forbearance, to substitute acceptance for judgment and exclusion, is an injunction the church at all times and in all places ought to heed, regardless of the particular matters in dispute. Our calling is to studiously seek to prevent the divisions that so easily follow from our failure to love and accept our brothers and sisters—for whom Christ also died—whose consciences on a disputable matter are different from our own.

AMANDA: I'm not sure that the dispute between the omnivores and the vegetarians is of the same order of magnitude as our differences about homosexuality and same-sex relationships. I'm sorry, folks. I just cannot see myself being part of a congregation where same-sex weddings are an accepted practice and where same-sex "married" couples are in positions of leadership and authority in such a congregation.

PHILIP: It might be too much of a challenge for any individual congregation to be pluralistic on this issue. I can certainly appreciate Amanda's feelings, and I want to be sensitive to her and others who feel the way she does. That could be "a bridge too far" for them. Perhaps a better solution would be to allow uniformity at the level of individual congregations and pluralism at the level of districts or denominations. A congregant could then choose to affiliate with either an affirming or a non-affirming congregation within the denomination. The denominational leadership group would then permit and promote pluralism within its organizational structure, and its leaders would be required to refrain from either promoting or opposing the interests of one side over those of the other in matters that affect the denomination as a whole.

DAVID: There are in fact a number of denominations that already practice this kind of pluralism on other issues. For example, I know of some denominations that permit but do not require their affiliated congregations to be open to having women pastors and elders. Some of these congregations oppose the inclusion of women in these leadership positions, while others oppose their exclusion. All are free to practice their own convictions on this matter internally, but are asked to exercise the kind of "forbearance" Stephanie brought up just now in regard to other congregations in the denomination that hold different convictions and follow different practices.

AMANDA: For me it would certainly be less stressful to belong to a congregation that is non-affirming even if it were part of a denomination that allowed both, than to be in a congregation that would require me to tolerate a practice that I believe to be against God's will.

DAVID: Not all denominations allow such congregational autonomy. Many are organized in a way that decisions of this order are made by a self-perpetuating hierarchy, and others hold that such decisions are to be made by deliberative representative assemblies meeting annually. In both these cases the decisions become binding on individual member congregations.

PHILIP: Doesn't that restrict the consciences of those individual congregations that feel constrained to follow a different path?

STEPHANIE: The balance between congregational autonomy and denominational authority is tricky, and different Christian denominations strike that balance differently. This too continues to be a matter of debate, and that is one reason we have so many Christian denominations.

DAVID: Well, we'll have to leave it there. Does anyone have a final question or comment?

STEPHANIE: We've navigated a lot of territory these last weeks, and I for one am pretty exhausted. I think we can agree that we've all learned a lot from each other. It would be interesting to hear from each of us just how we've been affected by the back and forth among us, but we'll have to leave that for another day. I'm grateful for all I've learned from each of you. Above all, I'm grateful for the sustaining guidance of the Holy Spirit throughout this process. God's Spirit has allowed us to maintain respect and friendship with one another despite our differences of viewpoint. I have gotten to know you better and love you more. For me, that's been the biggest take-away. May I end with a prayer of thanksgiving? *All murmur agreement. Stephanie continues.*

> *Father God, we don't know how to thank you for keeping our conversations on track, for giving us listening ears and open minds and hearts to hear your word and one another. Even though we did not reach agreement, Lord, help us to continue to respect and love one another and to wear our disagreements lightly. And we pray that Christians everywhere will by your grace do the same. In Jesus's name, Amen.*

Discussion Questions on Dialogue 4½

1. Stephanie makes a plea for "forbearance," the idea that Christians ought to give one another space to hold differing convictions on the subject of faithful, monogamous, same-sex relationships. Amanda finds herself unable to agree with Stephanie. Do you find such forbearance attractive or threatening?

2. Have your views about homosexuality and same-sex relationships and marriage changed as a result of studying these dialogues? If so, how they have changed? If not, why haven't they changed?

Epilogue

STEPHANIE: Thanks for listening in on our conversations. By now you will have plenty of questions of your own. We urge you to continue to pursue answers, to engage in dialogue, especially with people who don't necessarily share your point of view. We also hope that you will continue to read and to reflect on whatever you read, and above all to pray for the Spirit's guidance. I've asked Amanda, Dave, and Phil to join me in recommending some resources for further reading to you. As you might expect, each of us recommends items for further study that are aligned with our individual points of view. So I list them here.

Amanda's recommendations:

Allberry, Sam. *Is God Anti-gay? (Questions Christians Ask)*. Epsom, UK: The Good Book Company, 2013.

Burk, Denny, and Heath Lambert. *Transforming Homosexuality*. Phillipsburg, NJ: P&R, 2015.

Gagnon, Robert A. J. *The Bible and Homosexual Practice: Texts and Hermeneutics*. Nashville, TN: Abingdon, 2002.

"Nashville Statement." https://cbmw.org/nashville-statement/.

Philip's recommendations:

DeFranza, Megan K. "Journeying from the Bible to Christian Ethics in Search of Common Ground." In *Two Views on Homosexuality, the Bible and the Church*, edited by Preston Sprinkle, 69–101. Grand Rapids: Zondervan, 2016.

Lee, Justin. *Torn: Rescuing the Gospel from the Gays vs. Christians Debate*. New York: Jericho, 2012.

Keen, Karen R. *Scripture, Ethics and the Possibility of Same-sex Relationships*. Grand Rapids: Eerdmans, 2018.

Vines, Matthew. *God and the Gay Christian: The Biblical Case in Support of Same-Sex Relationships*. New York: Convergent, 2014.

"Reformation Project." https://reformationproject.org.

David's recommendations:

Hill, Wesley. *Spiritual Friendship: Finding Love in the Church as a Celibate Gay Christian.* Grand Rapids: Brazos, 2015.
————. *Washed and Waiting: Reflections on Christian Faithfulness and Homosexuality* (expanded edition). Grand Rapids: Zondervan, 2016.
Sprinkle, Preston. *People to be Loved: Why Homosexuality is not Just an Issue.* Grand Rapids: Zondervan, 2015.
"Spiritual Friendship." https://spiritualfriendship.org.

Stephanie's recommendations:

Albert, Nathan. *Embracing Love: My Journey to Hugging a Man in his Underwear.* Canton, MI: Read the Spirit, 2016.
Loader, William. "Homosexuality and the Bible." In *Two Views on Homosexuality, the Bible and the Church,* edited by Preston Sprinkle, 17–48. Grand Rapids: Zondervan, 2016.
Marin, Andrew. *Love is an Orientation: Elevating the Conversation with the Gay Community.* Downers Grove, IL: InterVarsity, 2009.
Otto, Tim. *Oriented to Faith: Transforming the Conflict over Gay Relationships.* Eugene, OR: Cascade, 2014.
Vanderwal–Gritter, Wendy. *Generous Spaciousness: Responding to Gay Christians in the Church.* Grand Rapids: Brazos, 2014.
"Oriented to Faith." http://orientedtofaith.com/.

Oh, by the way, a couple of weeks after we sent the manuscript off, David, Amanda, and I each received an invitation to Phil's wedding. Dave and I are going. Dave said that he's told Phil that by attending he is not endorsing Phil's marriage, but he does want to come and show his friendship and support for him. Amanda really struggled with the invitation. She finally decided that she couldn't go. She didn't want to just fill out and send in the response card enclosed with the invitation, but she knew it would be hard to tell Phil in person. So she asked me to come with her for moral support.

We met Phil on the café terrace by the campus library. Holding back tears, Amanda walked up to him. He stood up to greet her as she let the words tumble out. He looked at her, held out his arms and enfolded her. Then the tears came flooding—from both of them. They held each other for what seemed like an endless moment. I stood transfixed, my own eyes brimming with tears. Here were two of my very best friends, both of them gay, and both deeply committed followers of Jesus, with very different convictions about how to live out their lives, both equally convinced that they are following God's path for their lives. The moment is seared in my memory forever. I had no idea that these two were so attached to each other. The pain in both their hearts was palpable.

The pain of Jesus.